The Chartered Institute of Management Accountants

The Chartered Institute of Management Accountants
CIMA
Publishing

International Transfer Pricing

A Study of Cross-border Transactions

J Elliott
University of Southampton

C R Emmanuel
University of Glasgow

This publication arises from the research project 'A field study investigation of international transfer pricing (ITP) policy in twelve organisations' which was funded with a research grant from the CIMA Research Foundation. The award of a Research Foundation grant, and the publication of findings in this format, indicates that the recipient has successfully passed two separate peer review processes, which also involved practitioner assessors. The views expressed in this publication are the authors' own, and do not necessarily represent those of CIMA.

Acknowledgements

We should like to thank the Research Foundation of the Chartered Institute of Management Accountants for supporting this project. We also wish to record our gratitude to the managers and directors who spared the time to participate in the fieldwork and who discussed their international transfer-pricing policies in detail. The researchers are also indebted to Mrs Veda Smillie who painstakingly transformed numerous files and notes into a legible and articulate report.

First published in 2000 by:
The Chartered Institute of Management Accountants
63 Portland Place
London
W1N 4AB

ISBN 1 85971 346 7

Contents

Executive Summary

The current situation

Consistent with the worldwide trend, UK transfer-pricing legislation is currently being modernised. For accounting periods ending on or after 1 July 1999, transfer pricing falls within the corporate tax self-assessment system, which means that taxpayers must be able to demonstrate the use of arm's-length prices. Arm's-length prices include not just transaction-based methods, such as comparable uncontrolled price, resale price minus and full cost plus, but also profit-based methods such as the transactional net margin method (TNMM) and the profit-split method. Other changes include the introduction of advance pricing agreements (APAs), which encompass sophisticated risk–return profiles within functional analysis, increased power to penalise non-compliance, and increased documentation requirements.

These developments in themselves may be regarded as of limited interest to management accountants until it is realised that they relate to international transfer pricing (ITP) – the monetary value attaching to goods, services and intangibles traded between units of the same group which cross national boundaries. The annual value of such transactions is extremely difficult to gauge, but in the mid-1990s, the United Nations Conference on Trade and Development (UNCTAD) estimated that there were 44,500 multinational enterprises (MNEs) worldwide, with 275,000 foreign affiliates. In 1994, the assets of all foreign affiliates' assets were placed at $8.4 trillion: annual foreign direct investment in 1996 was $350 billion, the UK being the second-largest outward investor ($54 billion) at that time. As a consequence, the intra-group cross-border transactions in total constitute a significant proportion of world trade, which in some industries is even more pronounced. For example, the percentages of intra-group to all cross-border trade in automotive parts, pharmaceuticals, computing and electronics are estimated (Dunning and Pearce, 1985) to be in excess of 50 per cent of all exports in these sectors.

For management accountants, ITP resurrects the thorny issues of cash-flow management, the funding of investments overseas, the evaluation of subsidiaries and their managers, and effective tax management. Within this arena, marketing specialists, behavioural scientists, corporate strategists, tax lawyers, brand lawyers, economists and consultants can all claim a legitimate perspective on ITP. It is of little wonder that academic researchers have not produced a universally acceptable theory of ITP.

Instead, numerous surveys have been conducted which, over a 40-year period, have failed to uncover explanations of practice or to reveal patterns of association between ITP and multifarious variables. One of the problems relates to the differing focus that each survey has adopted. For example, is ITP addressed as the typical, on average or most frequently used process within the group, inter-subsidiary or between headquarters and subsidiaries? More recently, in the USA especially, research to detect evidence of income shifting has been undertaken, using financial accounting databases or confidential tax data. The tax influence is the prior assumption on which these studies are based, and alternative explanations of ITP in practice are largely ignored.

Theoretical frameworks suggested by Eccles (1985), Spicer (1988) and Colbert and Spicer (1995) are confined to domestic transfer-pricing situations. Nevertheless, the focus on transaction costs that the last authors in particular have offered prompted this current study, which places emphasis on one specific intra-group transaction that crosses national boundaries. Patterns which emerge at this micro-level of analysis may provide insights into ITP in the MNE or even industry sector.

Focus of the study

Each participant was asked to describe ITP for an individual, specific cross-border intra-group transaction of their choice. The fieldwork therefore involved face-to-face interviews which were subsequently fed back by means of reports for authentication and accuracy. By this means, we intended to gain in-depth understanding of the single transaction, while recognising that other transactions within the same MNE may not share the same ITP process or methods. Great caution must therefore apply to any apparently general comments emanating from the study.

The participating MNEs were not selected randomly. All twelve indicated a willingness to discuss ITP in an earlier survey (Elliott, 1998), and for this reason the views expressed are those offered by tax managers or directors of MNEs. The normal conditions of anonymity apply, resulting in each company being recognised by number only (Appendix 1).

The fieldwork therefore relates to five MNEs in financial services, four MNEs whose main activities are the manufacture and supply of products, and three MNEs whose main activities are the provision of services. In all but two cases the participants chose to describe a specific transaction relating to main activities. The parent company is in the UK in five instances, and in the USA for seven of the MNEs. Further details of the MNEs participating in the fieldwork research and those in the prior survey are displayed in Chapter 2.

The questionnaire responses to the prior survey allowed the researchers some familiarity with each MNE's ITP policies. A protocol was developed to prompt participants to place in context the specific ITP they had chosen to describe. This included broad questions on organisational structure, implementation and review of ITP policy, managerial evaluation and reward at the subsidiary or business-unit level, relationships with fiscal authorities, the use made of advisers and the levels of assurance sought to comply with tax legislation. In the majority of the interviews, these provided merely a checklist in order that all participants had the opportunity to discuss the same issues. Normally, the free flow of dialogue in the interviews meant that the issues were addressed naturally and without prompting.

Findings

Strategy and ITP

It proved impossible for our participants to describe a single intra-group transaction in isolation from the group's operations as a whole. In virtually all instances, commercial reality required the interconnectedness of the parts of the group to be recounted. For the financial services MNEs, the market was either global (for example, foreign exchange option trading or non-US-dollar swap derivatives) or displayed sequential interdependence, units in one part of the world generating clients for work to be executed by another part of the group located elsewhere. The latter incorporated investment management and corporate finance transactions.

For MNEs whose main activities involved the manufacture and distribution of products, commercial reality led to an emphasis on either a global marketing strategy or a global vertical-integration strategy. These strategies appear to influence the need for central purchasing, marketing and/or research and development. Inevitably, two forms of ITP were acknowledged: one relating to the physical flows of intermediate and final products, the other relating to the knowledge flows associated with royalties for intellectual property, brands or licences.

The services-providing MNEs appear to follow a type of cost-leadership strategy. Headquarter services are subject to cost-sharing arrangements unless the provision adds value when a mark-up is applied. In one instance, there is evidence of overseas investment in a low-cost, well-educated location to improve competitive advantage in global tendering for business. In all instances, the internal market is an important factor.

This last submission extends to all twelve of the MNEs. Whether the strategy emphasises a global marketing strategy or global vertical integration or global quality of service provision, ITP is centrally determined. Particularly in terms of the individual transactions relating to the MNEs' main activities, the decision to sell or purchase external of the group is not delegated to subsidiaries. This suggests that strategy influences the ITP process.

However, the discussions with some of the MNEs, especially those in the financial services and pharmaceutical sectors, indicated the influence that regulated environments exert on strategy. These, in turn, influenced internal structures and the flow of transactions.

ITP and strategy

It is possible that the strategy–ITP association is two-directional. The centrally determined ITP may be adjusted in response to market or fiscal changes. Certain of the participating MNEs mentioned exceptions to the accepted ITP policy when subsidiaries are in a start-up situation or are smaller units with limited facilities and product ranges. Other exceptions relate to foreign tax credits not being fully used or tax holidays would otherwise be lost. These examples suggest that the dynamics of specific countries or regions result in ITP being adjusted which, in turn, may lead to a more fundamental reappraisal of strategy. Internal structures develop to cater for these dynamic changes, such as the establishment of a commercial unit to arbitrate ITP adjustments between subsidiaries. Alternatively, systems are introduced to distinguish managerial and subsidiary performance when ITP adjustments may benefit group global performance but disadvantage one subsidiary.

In this last respect, the link between managerial rewards and subsidiary performance appears to be decoupled almost completely in the financial services MNEs. Internal reporting is concerned with the relative profitability of distinct global services and, as all subsidiaries may contribute to each service in a given time period, individual office or trader performance is extremely difficult to measure. Indeed, bonuses are determined by each level of management and individual rewards take into account the marketability of individual traders.

Amelioration systems are employed in the product- and service-provision MNEs: managerial performance and rewards are aggregated to a regional not country basis; profit-relief systems apply when apparent underachievement, in terms of profitability or cash flow at the subsidiary level, nevertheless benefits the group; alternative performance indicators are employed for specific subsidiaries; reporting for legal and taxation purposes is distinguished from evaluating subsidiary and managerial performance.

In total, these responses to the application of a centrally determined ITP convey an impression of the ways different MNEs accommodate the vagaries of changing market conditions and attempt to maintain managerial motivation. One interpretation of the relationships is that:

- MNE strategy determines ITP policy;
- dynamic market conditions, and changes in regulations and tax laws result in exceptions to the general ITP policy;
- with exceptions becoming more frequent, internal structures and systems are introduced to maintain subsidiary managerial commitment and motivation;
- dependent on the internal structures and systems capability to handle ITP adjustments effectively, strategy is reappraised and a different policy adopted.

Fiscal authority influence

Into this already complex labyrinth now appears the modernised tax laws which globally require MNEs to ensure that arm's-length prices are used and to maintain detailed documentation of their ITP for intra-group transactions.

Many of the twelve participating MNEs have well-established internal tax departments, some with significant staffing levels and expertise in ITP. Our meetings revealed, in some instances, regular contacts being maintained with fiscal authorities. One MNE has an office at headquarters for an Internal Revenue Service (IRS) inspector. The ability to interact with the fiscal authorities appears to be of mutual benefit. The authority may receive annual listings of all intra-group cross-border transactions, while MNE tax personnel may receive informal advice on future ITP policy in specific cases. Our fieldwork sample may be biased, in this respect, because of the immense size of some of the participating MNEs, and the length of time they have experienced contact with the fiscal authorities. In most cases, a willingness to participate in the study coincided with a certain degree of confidence that their transfer pricing policies would be upheld by the tax authorities.

This mutual compatibility is not illustrated, however, in the MNEs' perceptions of advance pricing agreements (APAs). A wide range of views is evident, as is experience of the process whereby an APA is obtained. There are instances where one MNE withdrew from the APA process, where others would prefer to argue after rather than before the event or transaction, and where satisfaction is expressed of the process and the subsequent operation of the APA. No association of these views with industry sector, parent company nationality, size or type of transaction appears to be merited.

What is apparent is that even MNEs with experience of fiscal authority reviews and audits and established internal tax departments are looking to strengthen their ITP expertise further. External advisers such as specialist, big-five accounting firm consultants, tax lawyers and economists well versed in functional analysis, are increasingly in demand. Similarly, there is demand for the services of former tax inspectors with ITP experience.

ITP methods

From this mêlée of strategic issues, internal structure, managerial reward and fiscal experience and expertise, it is surprising to report some consistency in the transfer-pricing methods employed. The preferred ITP methods for the chosen transactions are:

- in financial services MNEs, profit split;
- in manufacturing MNEs, standard full cost plus mark-up and resale price minus;
- in service-providing MNEs, actual cost and actual cost plus mark-up.

The one instance where a participating MNE described a negotiated ITP, justified by the comparable uncontrolled price method, remains under review with the relevant fiscal authority.

The consistency of the choice of method relative to the type of transaction or industry sector does not necessarily reflect the same adoption of strategy, structures and systems by MNEs in the same industry sector. In fact, the opposite may be the case. Obviously, there is a real opportunity for future research to address this issue.

Future trends and issues

At a practical level, there is:

- A need to recognise that cost of compliance with tax regulations varies with the type of transaction: product manufacturers in particular have the dual concern of documenting and justifying ITP and royalty agreements.
- A need for fiscal authorities and MNEs to share information on their perspec-

tives of national tax liability and global commerciality: this may in time educate both sides to comprehend the complexities of global transactions with some supranational body, perhaps the EU Arbitration Convention or a revised OECD Double Taxation Convention model, mediating disputes.

- A need for the fiscal authorities to be resourced to match expertise in ITP methods with specific industry sectors: this may prove to be of mutual benefit in forging understanding and ensuring that APAs or some similar arrangements are used effectively.

From the theoretical perspective, the interaction and direction of the influence of strategy and ITP is highlighted as a potentially fundamental area of future investigation. This cannot be examined in any meaningful way without the co-operation of MNEs. It is therefore appropriate that we end by acknowledging our thanks to the twelve MNEs who participated in this study.

1

The Significance of International Transfer Pricing

1.1 Introduction

There is no doubt that international transfer pricing (ITP) is one of the most important international tax issues facing multinational enterprises (MNEs) in the operation of their global businesses. The 1994 OECD Transfer Pricing Guidelines recognised that the rapid growth in MNEs' global business has meant that both MNEs themselves and fiscal authorities need to pay greater attention to how an MNE's global taxable profit is shared across all the tax jurisdictions in which it operates.

The magnitude of the problem is apparent when considering the importance of foreign direct investment (FDI) to the world economy. UNCTAD (1997a) shows that in the mid-1990s there were about 44,500 MNEs worldwide, with over 275,000 foreign affiliates. UNCTAD (1997b) also stated that the value of goods and services of foreign affiliates are now greater than exports and appear to be the principal means for delivering goods and services to foreign markets. The value of foreign affiliates' worldwide assets were $8.4 trillion in 1994. On a global basis, UNCTAD (1997a) estimated that both global FDI inflows and outflows were just under $350 billion in 1996. The two largest outward investors were the USA ($85 billion) and the UK ($54 billion). The two largest recipient countries of inward investment were the USA ($85 billion) and China ($41 billion).

Given the huge sums of money passing between affiliates in an MNE, fiscal authorities are particularly keen to ensure that they capture their fair share of an MNE's global tax liability. This focus on tax take has led the USA to tighten its rules and regulations on international transfer pricing. In turn, other countries have introduced new or modified transfer-pricing rules to protect their tax revenues. The impetus for the more onerous regime in the USA is explained by Laster and McCauley (1994):

> ... the scant profit of foreign firms operating in the United States has emerged as one of the biggest puzzles in international finance. That 4.7 million workers using $1.8 trillion in assets to generate sales of $1.2 trillion could fail to turn a profit strikes many as unbelievable. Could foreign companies have paid $316 billion in the past decade for firms earning $10.7 billion in the year before acquisition only to lose money overall on their holdings in 1992 – a year in which US-owned firms earned record profits? (p. 44)

Despite the importance of taxation on ITP decisions, one must also recognise that there are a host of other potentially influential factors. For instance, Abdallah (1989) set out nine objectives for establishing an ITP policy: reduction of income taxes; reduction of tariffs; minimisation of foreign exchange risks; avoidance of a conflict with host countries' governments; management of cash flows; competitiveness; performance evaluation; motivation; goal congruence. The problem with establishing an ITP policy is that it is not possible to satisfy all these different objectives. Indeed, many of these objectives are competing influences. Leitch and Barrett (1992) reviewed the transfer pricing literature and concluded that:

> MNEs often have many objectives whose achievement depends on situation-specific factors.... The majority of these factors are motivated by MNE, FDI and organisational theory. Because they are often so closely interrelated ... many of these objectives conflict and are difficult to rank in spite of what surveys may indicate. These difficulties are indicative of the complexity surrounding the multinational transfer-pricing element. (pp. 67–8)

One of the main objectives of this study is to understand how important these different factors are in relation to one specific cross-border intra-group transaction selected by each of the twelve MNEs.

This opening chapter proceeds as follows. First, the empirical evidence of ITP is considered. Second, recent fiscal developments are described for selected countries and for the OECD. Finally, some theoretical foundations are introduced and then the current position is evaluated.

1.2 Empirical evidence

There have been numerous reviews of the transfer-pricing literature which attempt to evaluate and synthesise the empirical evidence (Leitch and Barrett, 1992; McAulay and Tomkins, 1992; Giovannini et al., 1993; Emmanuel and Mehafdi, 1994; Mehafdi and Emmanuel, 1997). One of the overwhelming conclusions is that ITP is complex, multidisciplinary, and remains a puzzle. These studies leave us with an overwhelming view that over 40 years of theoretical and empirical research has provided us with a limited understanding ITP within MNEs and that an alternative approach to ITP research is required.

1.2.1 Economics

Hirshleifer (1956) proved that the efficient transfer price should be the marginal cost of the selling division at the optimal output level. Subsequent theoretical papers have attempted to improve the economic models (see Rugman and Eden, 1985) by, for instance, considering the design and optimality of a set of transfer-pricing rules and regulations from different perspectives (e.g. when one country imposes the dominant rules). However, these theoretical findings do not necessarily hold in the 'real world'. For instance, tax and tariff distortions, interest rates and exchange controls, and other market imperfections are just some of the situations in which theoretically efficient transfer prices do not hold. Furthermore, managers must deal with all aspects of a problem when determining transfer prices and cannot conveniently ignore key variables discarded by a particular theory (Eccles, 1985).

1.2.2 *Tax*

There have been a number of studies which analyse either confidential tax data (Grubert and Mutti, 1991; Collins and Shackelford, 1998) or financial accounting databases (Harris, 1993; Klassen et al., 1993; Jacob, 1996) to investigate international transfer-pricing issues. These studies are mainly restricted to the USA, owing to problems of access and information disclosure limitations in other countries. The findings of these studies are not too compelling because the explanations are limited to the influences of tax, alternative explanations are not considered, and the suitability of the underlying data is questionable.

1.2.3 *Surveys*

Mehafdi and Emmanuel (1997) review over 70 transfer-pricing studies over a 40-year period and conclude that transfer-pricing research is too complex to lend itself to survey research methods. The main limitation is that survey-based research has not improved our understanding of transfer pricing sufficiently – it has merely highlighted the gap between theory and practice. Leitch and Barrett (1992) question the usefulness of the style of typical survey questions because of the uniqueness of each MNE's environments.

1.3 Recent fiscal developments

1.3.1 *The current position*

Since the mid-1980s, the USA has been the prime instigator of the introduction of more onerous and punitive transfer-pricing rules and regulations, culminating in the s482 Final Regulations which were released on 1 July 1994[1] (US, 1994).[2] At the same time the OECD revised its own draft guidelines. Since then the OECD and the USA have been refining their guidelines and regulations, respectively, and many fiscal authorities around the world have responded by introducing their own transfer-pricing rules and regulations.

Deloitte Touche Tohmatsu (1999) summarised the current transfer-pricing position for selected countries as of 1 January 1999. Table 1.1 gives selected extracts for the OECD, Australia, Japan, the UK and the USA. The first two rows present the tax authority (i.e. the name of the fiscal authority) and the regulations, rulings and guidelines which are applicable in each country. The third row demonstrates how onerous the documentation requirements are becoming globally and how important it is that MNEs should be able to support their transfer-pricing policies with the appropriate documentation. The fourth row illustrates the variety of requirements concerning the transfer-pricing information which should be disclosed on the tax return. In relation to disclosure, the UK is the least onerous, but there is a presumption that all transactions are at arm's length and can be supported.

---

1 They were published in the Federal Register on 8 July 1994.

2 Revisiting the confounding objectives faced by MNEs, Borkowski (1992b) argued that 'an MNC must balance choosing the transfer-pricing method that is optimal for the company's operating environment with the requirements of s482 (the IRS's regulations governing transfer pricing)' (p. 67).

Table 1.1: Transfer-pricing issues in selected countries (extract from Deloitte Touche Tohmatsu (1999))

	OECD	Australia	Japan	UK	USA
Tax authority	Not applicable	Australian Tax Office	National Tax Administration	Inland Revenue	Internal Revenue Service
Regulations, rulings guidelines	Transfer Pricing Guidelines for Multinational Enterprises and Tax Administrations*	Final Rulings (TR 92/11, TR 94/14, TR 95/23, TR 97/20, TR 98/11, TR 98/16, TR 1999/1) Draft Rulings (TR 95/D11, TR 95/D31, TR 97/D5)†	STML–Enforcement Order 39-12 STML–Circular 66-4-1 – 66-4-9	Sch. 28AA, Taxes Act of 1988‡	Reg s1.482§ Reg s1.6662–6#
Documentation requirement	Pricing decisions should be documented in accordance with prudent business practices Reasonable for tax authorities to expect taxpayers to prepare and maintain such material No contemporaneous obligation	Document pricing decisions in accordance with prudent business practices Certain documents required Documentation contemporaneous with transaction preferred	No statutory requirements, but strongly recommended for audit defence No contemporaneous obligation	Taxpayers should keep records needed to deliver a correct and complete return In practice, burden shifting to taxpayer to demonstrate reasonable transfer pricing Certain documents are required to be prepared and retained Contemporaneous documentation is expected.	Must include certain principal documents, as well as supporting documents Contemporaneous documentation required
Tax return disclosures	Should be limited to information sufficient to allow tax administration to determine which taxpayers need further examination	Schedule 25A requires disclosure of types of transactions, dollar amounts, countries involved, documentation maintained and methodologies used	Schedule 16-4: Detailed Statement Concerning Foreign Affiliated Persons	No separate disclosure required (i.e. on signing tax return taxpayer will be implicity confirming compliance with arm's-length standard)	Forms 5471 and 5472 require disclosure of detailed information on controlled transactions with foreign entities

* OECD: Various chapters published at July 1995, March 1996 and October 1997.
† Australia: All draft and final rulings have retroactive effect to 1982.
‡ UK: This is new legislation which applies to all accounting periods starting after 1 July 1998.
§ USA: Effective for tax years beginning after 6 October 1994.
# USA: Effective 9 February 1996.

In 1998, the UK transfer-pricing legislation, which had been in place for nearly 50 years, was 'modernised'. In brief, for accounting periods ending on or after 1 July 1999, transfer pricing falls within the corporate tax self-assessment system. This means that taxpayers are required to ensure that their computation of taxable profits reflects arm's-length prices; taxpayers are required to justify the transfer-pricing policy; taxpayers are required to maintain sufficient and appropriate contemporaneous documentation[3] (see Table 1.1); and penalties might apply to certain tax adjustments based on non-arm's-length pricing.[4] In 1999, new legislation allows for advance pricing agreements (APAs) to be agreed between taxpayers and the Inland Revenue. As stated in Inland Revenue (1999),[5] 'APAs can assist taxpayers by providing certainty in situations where their cross-border activities raise particularly complex or difficult transfer-pricing issues.' Prior to the new legislation, APAs were only available in the UK under the mutual agreement procedure of double tax agreements.

1.3.2 Acceptable transfer-pricing methods

Table 1.2 illustrates acceptable transfer-pricing methods and the priority of these methods in the selected countries. The OECD has set out details of a range of acceptable transaction-based methods and profit-based methods.

Transaction-based methods

Transaction-based methods 'compare the prices charged in controlled transactions undertaken between those enterprises with prices charged in comparable transactions undertaken between independent enterprises' (para. 91). OECD (1994) identified three transaction-based methods:

- **Comparable uncontrolled price (CUP).** The CUP method is the most direct determination of an arm's-length price. This method refers to the sales price between unrelated buyers and sellers for a comparable transaction. Ideally the circumstances should be identical, but some latitude is allowed to compare with a non-identical CUP (e.g. differences in the terms or timing of the transaction) and make an appropriate adjustment. One of the main problems associated with this method is that it is often very difficult for companies to access data on transactions between 'unrelated buyers and sellers'.

---

3 The October 1998 issue of the Inland Revenue's *Tax Bulletin* (issue 37) provides some guidance on the documentation that needs to be maintained in the UK.

4 The December 1998 issue of the Inland Revenue's *Tax Bulletin* (issue 38) provides some guidance on penalties in the UK. The bulletin states that 'The Revenue recognises that the issue of penalties on transfer-pricing adjustments will be a sensitive one, especially in the early years of the new regime. As a result, and to ensure that a consistent approach is taken across the department, all potential penalty cases will be monitored by International Division, working in conjunction with Compliance Division.'

5 Inland Revenue (1999), 'Advance Pricing Agreements (APAs)', Inland Revenue Press Release 87/99, 31 March 1999.

Table 1.2: Transfer-pricing methods in selected countries (extract from Deloitte Touche Tohmatsu (1999))

	OECD	Australia	Japan	UK	USA
Acceptable methods	CUP, resale price, cost plus, profit split (e.g. contribution analysis or residual analysis), TNMM	CUP, resale price, cost plus, profit split (e.g. contribution analysis or residual analysis), TNMM	CUP, resale price, cost plus, other methods (e.g. profit split)	CUP, resale price, cost plus, profit split (e.g. residual analysis), TNMM	CUP, resale price, cost plus, comparable profit split, residual profit split, CPM
Priority of methods	Reasonable method Transaction-based preferred over profit-based	Most appropriate method Transaction-based preferred over profit-based	Transaction-based methods preferred over profit-based methods	Most reasonable method Transaction-based preferred over profit based	Best method

- **Resale price.** The resale price method determines the arm's-length price by taking the actual price at which goods are sold by a reseller and deducting a normal profit margin which would be obtained from transactions with unrelated parties. Any difference between the related transaction and the unrelated transaction should be reflected by an adjustment to the normal profit margin.
- **Cost-plus.** The cost-plus method takes the cost of production and adds the appropriate gross profit margin. Again, this mark-up should be determined by reference to the mark-up earned by a manufacturer's sales to unrelated parties for the same/similar transactions.

Profit-based methods

Profit-based methods 'examine the profits that arise from controlled transactions of one or more of the associated enterprises participating in those transactions' (para. 130). Two methods are identified:

- **Comparable profits method (CPM)/transactional net margin method (TNMM).** The CPM refers to the profit levels earned by uncontrolled parties which are considered comparable based on acceptable criteria, such as location, size and line of business. Any differences between the companies being compared should be taken into account.

  CPM has been a source of disagreement between the USA and the OECD. As a result, the OECD removed any reference to CPM in its most recent guidelines, and introduced the TNMM and listed it as a transactional profit method. Stitt (1995) argued that

  > ... some commentators have suggested that TNMM is nothing more than CPM with a new name, except that more emphasis is placed on information about the company under review, rather than industry averages or other data not linked directly to particular transactions. (p. 94)

The main difference between the two approaches is that TNMM uses net margin measures (e.g. return on sales) to compare controlled and uncontrolled *transactions,* whereas CPM uses measures of operating profitability (e.g. rate of return) to compare the profitability of controlled and uncontrolled *parties* (using an entire company or business segment).

- **Profit-split method**. The profit-split method splits the total profit earned between the two related parties using an equitable formula (e.g. in proportion to capital employed). This method should compare the split with profit splits between unrelated parties, but as this information is rarely available an equitable means of division should be found.

Use of transaction-based and profit-based methods

GAO (1995) provided some details about the relative use of these methods. For those transfer-pricing issues completed in the fiscal years 1990/92, the US IRS international examiners found that CUP had been used in 25 per cent of the cases, cost plus in 14 per cent, resale price in 12 per cent and other methods in 48 per cent (note rounding). As at 7 July 1994, 75 methods used in APAs could be disaggregated to CUP being used in 8 per cent of the cases, cost plus in 7 per cent, resale price in 23 per cent, profit measures in 19 per cent, formulary apportionment in 17 per cent and miscellaneous other allocation methods in 27 per cent (note rounding).

Deloitte Touche Tohmatsu (1998) commented on the 1995/96 Schedule 25A[6] statistics published by the Australian Tax Office (ATO). According to the information, 67 per cent of the 7,787 MNEs lodging a Schedule 25A were able to select and apply one of the recognised transactional-based methods (e.g. 2,220 used CUP and 1,300 used cost plus). However, instead of accepting that MNEs are applying the recommended methods, the ATO has questioned whether this high rate of compliance with accepted methods is actually plausible: 'the ATO's experience and efforts to date would suggest that the lack of available comparable data in Australia would not enable companies to apply these methods' (p. 1).

1.4 Theoretical foundations

Tang (1993) considers the multidisciplinary nature of transfer pricing in relation to its interfaces with selected disciplines: marketing; behavioural science; business policy; international business; economics and finance; law; taxation; and accounting. Therefore different commentators have explained transfer pricing in terms of different theoretical foundations. This section considers conceptual foundations based on theories of MNEs, asset specificity, and from a holistic viewpoint.

6 The Schedule 25A form is an additional (mandatory) tax return form that requires the identification and quantification of related party dealings.

1.4.1 *Multinational theories*

Leitch and Barrett (1992) contended that:

> ... the theory of MNEs argues that MNEs arise and engage in FDI in order to exploit imperfections in global markets. Although not explicitly motivated by this theory, the transfer-pricing literature is largely in harmony with this exploitation argument. (p. 84)

Indeed, a number of theories have been used to try to understand and explain FDI and MNE activity. For instance, Dunning's eclectic approach (Dunning, 1981, 1988) is an established paradigm for the conditions which determine the degree to which MNEs engage in FDI. The eclectic approach is so called because it builds on industrial organisation theory, location theory and market failure theory. According to Dunning (1980) there are three main determinants that dictate the likelihood of an enterprise engaging in international production through FDI, namely ownership, location and internalisation advantages (OLI advantages).

1.4.2 *Asset specificity*

Following the research by Spicer (1988), who incorporated the markets and hierarchies framework to develop nine hypotheses on transfer pricing, Colbert and Spicer (1995) have extended this research using multiple case studies. The rationale for the model is that analysis is conducted at the transaction level (rather than concentrating on the MNE in totality) and the transaction costs are determined by three dimensions. These dimensions are identified as:

- asset specificity – including physical assets, human assets, site specificity, and dedicated asset specificity (productive capacity);
- uncertainty;
- extent – frequency and volume of transactions.

In particular, Spicer (1988) argued that

> ... an organisational theory of the transfer-pricing process requires a wider consideration of relationships among a firm's diversification strategy, its intra-firm transactions, its organisation structure and its management accounting and control systems.

1.4.3 *Holistic*

More recently, some commentators have argued that it is necessary to take a more holistic view of transfer pricing within the MNE and the environment in which it operates. The context of ITP needs to be better understood. For instance, how does an MNE approach ITP? What is the corporate structure? What are the corporate strategies? What is the nature of the global market for the MNE?

Meer-Kooistra (1994) carried out case study research in four Dutch MNEs, leading to a greater in-depth knowledge about how transfer-pricing systems function. Two specific recommendations of this research reiterate the need for more attention to context:

> Insight into how internal transactions are co-ordinated requires further research into the entire relation between the parties concerned. Therefore, it is necessary to look at all stages of a transaction and at all elements of a transfer-pricing system. Also, it is necessary to look at the context in which transfer-pricing systems function, and to take into account the interaction with other co-ordination rules. (pp. 148–9)

> Research into the functioning of transfer-pricing systems has to take full account of the processes of change and adaptation, or the dynamics of the phenomenon. We need to remember that we are researching a real situation that has developed over the years due to decisions with long-term influence on the activities. Moreover, researching the formal regulations will not suffice. In addition, research into the real procedures is necessary. (p. 150)

Similarly, Mehafdi and Emmanuel (1997) have argued that:

> ... better insights into the complexities of this problem can be gained when the research methodology encompasses not only the technical aspects, but also the organisational and behavioural dimensions ... thus what is more important is whether the transfer-pricing system befits the strategic and structural circumstances of the particular company, and reflects the operational realities of the divisions involved in the internal trade.

However, little is available in terms of a theory of international transfer pricing.

1.5 Evaluation

This chapter has provided a flavour of the importance of ITP to both MNEs and fiscal authorities. With increasing levels of FDI and the increasing importance of MNEs in the global economy, fiscal authorities are protecting their tax revenues through more restrictive and onerous transfer-pricing rules and regulations. In turn, MNEs must commit greater resources to documenting and supporting their transfer-pricing policies to increase their levels of assurance that they will not be subject to penalties.

Previous studies, notably questionnaire surveys and income-shifting database studies, leave many questions unanswered concerning the way in which MNEs determine their transfer-pricing policies and which factors are truly influential. Therefore, it can be asserted with strong justification that the main objectives of current research into ITP in MNEs should be with a view to a deeper and richer understanding of the subject, to explore relationships, and to take a more holistic approach that considers the contextual setting of intra-group transactions. Case studies and fieldwork could fulfil this objective and it might also provide practitioners with a 'deeper and richer understanding of the social context in which they work and make them aware of the problems, and the possibilities for solutions' (Scapens, 1990, pp. 278–9). Furthermore, Emmanuel and Mehafdi (1998) have argued that ITP research studies need to focus on individual transactions and that it is important to place an intra-group transaction into its context within the MNE. This requires some consideration of the strategic, organisational and behavioural dimensions of the MNE.

2

The Sample

This study follows on from a CIMA-sponsored survey (Elliott, 1998) which set out to understand more about the way in which both UK groups and foreign groups approach international transfer pricing within the UK. The current study complements the previous findings by taking a more in-depth view and focusing on one specific cross-border intra-group transaction in each of twelve MNEs.

2.1 The earlier survey

The survey (Elliott, 1998) was sponsored by CIMA and supported by Deloitte & Touche. There were two mailings of the survey instrument to recipients of Deloitte & Touche's 'The Arm's Length Standard'[7] between November 1997 and March 1998. The main recipients of this publication included tax managers and finance directors. The survey was completed on a confidential and anonymous basis. At that time there were just under 400 names on the mailing list and in total 51 usable responses were received (about a 13 per cent response rate).

The survey instrument is shown in Appendix 2, and the general statistics and analysis of selected responses are presented in this chapter in terms of three out of the four sections of the survey:[8]

- organisational characteristics;
- transfer pricing – internal issues and dealings with tax authorities;
- transfer pricing policy reviews.

The survey instrument asked whether any companies would be willing to participate in a further study. Of the 51 respondents, 18 MNEs indicated a willingness to participate further and CIMA accepted a proposal to conduct a field study of 12 MNEs. The twelve interviews were conducted over the period April–June 1998. With two exceptions[9] the interviews were recorded and transcribed. With one exception the interviews were attended by both researchers. In all cases, a summary of the interview (by the researchers) was sent back to the interviewees for their comments, which were sought by follow-up telephone interviews. The agreed summaries are included

7 This is a regular newsletter containing transfer-pricing information prepared by Deloitte Touche Tohmatsu for international investors in major countries.

8 Each table is numbered in accordance with the question number on the survey instrument.

9 These two participants preferred that the interviews should not be recorded.

in Appendix 1. In all cases, each organisation's contribution is treated on a *strictly anonymous* basis to protect *confidentiality*.

Table 2.1 summarises some of the key information for the twelve participants. Each MNE is numbered in the order in which the interviews took place. This code number is used to identify the summary in Appendix 1 and to analyse the transaction in Chapters 3–6. Table 2.1 also shows the MNEs' main activity, the role of the main contact person, the number of interviewees attending each interview, the specific cross-border intra-group transaction, and whether or not the interview was recorded.

Table 2.1: Sample characteristics

Code no.	*Activity*	*Contact person (no. of interviewees)*	*Specific cross-border intra-group transaction*	*Tape-recorded*
1	Auto components	Tax manager (1)	Manufactured goods	Yes
2	Tobacco	Tax manager (1)	Manufactured goods	Yes
3	Oil extraction	Tax managers (3)	Service provision	No
4	Pharmaceuticals	Tax managers (2)	Manufactured goods	No
5	Financial sector	MD (1)	Financial services	Yes
6	Financial sector	Director (1)	Financial services	Yes
7	Financial sector	Tax manager (1)	Financial services	Yes
8	Financial sector	Tax manager (1)	Financial services	Yes
9	PR/advertising	Tax manager (1)	Service provision	Yes
10	Oil extraction	Tax managers (2)	Service provision	Yes
11	Financial sector	Tax manager (1)	Financial services	Yes
12	Engineering services	Tax manager (1)	Service provision	Yes

2.2 The participating organisations

The profiles of the twelve participants are illustrated in the tables below, and selected information is contrasted with the profile of the 51 respondents to the survey.[10] This information is based on earlier survey responses alone and incorporates none of the interview evidence at this stage. The findings of the twelve interviews are evaluated in Chapters 3–6.

2.2.1 Organisational characteristics

Question 1a analyses the respondents in terms of their level of sales. Although the interviewees range from small to very big, half of those MNEs interviewed have a turnover exceeding £5bn. There is no significant difference in the range of annual sales for the fieldwork companies and survey companies.

10 The following tables include all survey responses – in some cases, not all 51 respondents answered a particular question.

1a. What is the level of annual company sales?

Size of companies	*Fieldwork*	*Survey*
Less than £100m	1	9
£100–£250m	1	4
£250–£500m	1	5
£500–£1bn	2	6
£1–£2.5bn	1	4
£2.5–£5bn	0	6
Over £5bn	6	16

In the sample of interviewees there are five UK groups and seven US groups, which represent the main two nationalities in the survey sample.

1d. Nationality of parent company

Nationality	*Fieldwork*	*Survey*
UK	5	26
USA	7	15
Europe	0	7
Australia/Japan	0	3

The respondents were asked to identify the nature of their activity/activities (some respondents identifying more than one activity). The activities are illustrated for the UK and US companies only.

2. Nature of company's activity (activities)

Activity	*UK fieldwork*	*UK survey*	*USA fieldwork*	*USA survey*
Wholesaler	1	1	0	0
Distributor	0	0	1	4
Retailer	0	1	2	2
Manufacturer	2	12	2	5
Service company	0	3	2	4
R&D	1	1	0	1
Banking/investment	2	4	3	4
Computer software	0	1	0	0
Facilities management	0	1	0	0
Insurance	0	0	0	1
Media	0	1	0	0
Mining	0	1	0	0
Oil and gas	0	0	1	1
Public relations	1	1	0	0
Telecommunications	0	1	0	0
Utility	0	1	0	0

Looking at the interviewees' activities in more detail, the predominant international internal transactions as identified in the survey are illustrated.

4a. What is your single main/predominant type of international internal transaction?

Predominant international internal trade	*Fieldwork*	*Survey*
Product sales/finished goods/parts	3	16
Financial trades/derivatives/eurobond purchases and sales/security transactions/guarantees	5	7
Management fees/expense recharge/marketing/ product support/inter-company services	2	7
Financing	0	4
Royalties	0	3
Public relations	1	1
Distribution fee	0	1
Data products	0	1
Reinvoicing of hardware and software	0	1
Purchase of computer products	0	1
Sale of oil	1	1

The survey respondents were asked to identify the characteristics of their single main/predominant type of international internal trade. The profile of the twelve interviewees is illustrated and demonstrates that these are recurring, high-volume transactions with a certain degree of specific investment and certainty about the intra-group flows.

4b. What are the characteristics of your single main/predominant type of international internal transaction?

	Non-specific 1	*2*	*3*	*4*	*Highly specific* 5
Human/capital investment	1	0	3	2	5
	Occasional 1	*2*	*3*	*4*	*Recurring* 5
Frequency	0	0	0	3	9
	Very low 1	*2*	*3*	*4*	*Very high* 5
Volumes	1	0	2	2	7
	Very uncertain 1	*2*	*3*	*4*	*Very certain* 5
Levels of certainty	0	2	3	4	3

The respondents were asked to estimate the level of international internal trade as a percentage of total company sales. The eleven interviewees who estimated a figure all had proportions exceeding 1 per cent, and eight of these exceeded 10 per cent.

3. What is the proportion of international internal trade as a percentage of total company sales?

International internal trade	*Fieldwork*	*Survey*
Less than 1%	0	7
1–10%	3	20
10–25%	4	8
25–50%	3	8
Over 50%	1	5

2.2.2 Transfer pricing – internal issues and dealings with tax authorities

Question 10 asks whether each of goods, services, intangibles and financing are the main transfer-pricing issues in the company. The table illustrates that, for the interviewees, each activity receives a broad range of responses, i.e. from it never being an issue to always being an issue. The most frequent transfer-pricing issue for the twelve MNEs relates to services, for which nine of the interviewees consider services to be often/always an issue.

10. What are the main transfer pricing issues in your company?

	Never	*Infrequently*	*Sometimes*	*Often*	*Always*
Goods	3	2	0	0	4
Services	0	2	0	3	6
Intangibles	3	0	3	2	3
Financing	2	1	2	4	3

The interviewees ranked the different pricing methods in terms of applicability. The twelve interviewees demonstrate a range of most applicable methods.

13. Please identify the top pricing methods in order of applicability to your company.

	UK	*USA*
CUP	2	0
Resale price	1	1
Cost plus	1	3
Profit split	0	2
CPM	0	1
Cost allocation – separately agreed	1	0

The respondents ranked the top three factors in terms of their importance in determining the transfer price. The most important factors (featuring in the top three factors) for both the 12 interviewees and all 51 respondents are maximisation of global profit (identified by 6 and 16 respectively), aggressiveness of tax authority (5 and 13), simplicity and ease of use (4 and 15), stability of transfer price over time (4 and 13), and market penetration (3 and 13). These factors demonstrate the trade-offs which companies must consider when determining their transfer-pricing policies. Specifically, the decision can involve a recognition and ranking of the main drivers: profit management versus simplicity versus fiscal requirements/interest versus corporate strategy. One of the objectives of the interviews is to understand the relative importance of these features in relation to specific transactions.

16. Please rank the top three factors in order of importance to your company in determining the transfer price

	Ranking				
Factors	*1st*	*2nd*	*3rd*	*Fieldwork top 3*	*Survey top 3*
Competitive position of foreign subsidiary	1	0	0	1	8
Local market conditions	0	1	1	2	11
Maintain solvency of subsidiary	1	0	0	1	7
Market penetration	1	1	1	3	13
Parent cost recovery	1	1	0	2	8
Provide the parent with a fair return on assets	0	0	1	1	6
Simplicity and ease of use	1	2	1	4	15
Stability of transfer price over time	1	1	2	4	13
Subsidisation of infant foreign subsidiary	0	0	1	1	1
Aggressiveness of tax authority	1	1	3	5	13
Differentials in tax rates and tax legislation among countries	0	3	0	3	11
Maximisation of global profit	5	0	1	6	16
Protection against foreign exchange losses	0	1	0	1	4
Rate of customs duties and legislation	0	1	0	1	1
UK tax treatment of dividend remittances	0	0	1	1	2

2.2.3 *Transfer-pricing policy reviews*

As at the time of the survey (1997–8), most of the twelve interviewees had had either very recent or ongoing internal reviews of their transfer-pricing policy.

28. When did your company have its most recent (internal) transfer-pricing policy review?

International internal trade	*12 interviewees*	*All 51 responses*
Started 1992–3	0	1
1994	1	3
1995	0	2
1996	3	5
1997	2	12
1998	1	2
Continuous/constant	0	3
Current/ongoing	3	9
Ongoing APA	0	2

Finally, nine of the twelve interviewees had provided in their survey response some detailed information about what they considered to be the main problems and the main successes associated with the transfer-pricing policy review. If appropriate, these problems and successes (see table below) can be explored in more depth during the interviews.

Main problems encountered in the course of the most recent transfer-pricing policy review	*Main successes resulting from the most recent transfer-pricing policy review*
Getting overseas companies to accept charges; getting overseas tax authorities to accept	Inland Revenue acceptance of existing problem
Valuation of intangibles	Coherent and consistent policy group-wide
Complexity	Global certainty
No particular problems	Consensus
Substantiation of arm's-length price to satisfaction of tax authorities	Limited addition to taxable profits
No comparable arm's-length prices	Renegotiated APA
Realism of pricing	Implementation and reassurance from an external adviser
Deciding on roles of each party	Uniform policy with no exceptions
Uncertainty over the application of the widening of the financing criteria by the IR, especially with regard to parent company guarantees	Understanding how the recharge system works from other group companies for services

2.3 Focus on individual transactions

Recent attempts to gain insights and detect consensus from empirical studies based on surveys have met with little success (Borkowski, 1996). Yet UK legislative changes, OECD recommendations and continual fiscal interest worldwide make this a topical and contentious area worthy of research and a better understanding. The objective of the field study is to place each company's ITP policy for transactions within a rich organisational context to determine whether underlying patterns emerge.

More specifically, the field study investigates ITP for an individual *specific cross-border intra-group transaction* of the interviewee's choice in each of the twelve MNEs. Although these organisations span a large number of industries (including both financials and non-financials) and the nature of the specific transactions span manufactured goods, financial services and service provision, the field study provides a number of insights which might inform future research.

Spicer (1988) and Colbert and Spicer (1995) have conducted deductive and inductive analyses at the transaction level and investigated the transaction costs in terms of the dimensions of that transaction. However, the current research addresses two of the main limitations of this earlier research. First, their study is restricted to domestic transfer pricing, whereas this study introduces the international dimension. Second, although they acknowledge that a wider set of factors might be important considerations in setting a transfer-pricing policy (TPP), they have concentrated on an explanation based on three dimensions:

- asset specificity – including physical assets, human assets, site specificity, and dedicated asset specificity (productive capacity);
- uncertainty;
- extent – frequency and volume of transactions.

While the potential importance of these dimensions is recognised, ITP also requires consideration of fiscal regulations and actions, the evolution of corporate strategy and the dynamic changes occasioned by global markets.

At the early stages of the research study, a protocol was developed to provide prompts during the interviews. For the first few interviews the protocol proved to be a useful guide, but with increased experience it acted more as an *aide-mémoire*. In particular, the protocol provided prompts on issues such as organisational structure and context, the specific transaction in the market context, formulation and implementation of the transfer-pricing policy, performance evaluation and reward schemes, levels of assurance, relationships with fiscal authorities, relationships with advisers, and wider-ranging considerations such as the affect of the euro. In addition, the researchers used the survey responses to familiarise themselves before the interview. In some cases, the chosen cross-border intra-group transaction coincided with the survey responses. In other cases, the survey responses were not related to or did not help to contextualise the chosen cross-border intra-group transaction.

2.4 Strengths and limitations

The current study can be categorised as descriptive and/or exploratory field-based research (based on Spicer, 1992). However, it must be recognised that exploratory studies can be used as a basis for explaining accounting practice (Scapens, 1990). Once completed, Yin (1989) provides useful guidelines for judging whether or not the research represents an exemplary case study. For instance, Yin (1989) and Eisenhardt (1989) provide methodological guidance for satisfying construct validity, internal validity, external validity and reliability issues. These issues are satisfied for the proposed study as follows :

- *Construct validity* – made use of earlier questionnaire responses, designed a protocol, returned interview summaries to the participants, and engaged in follow-up discussions (over the phone) with the participants.
- *Internal validity* – this is inapplicable to the exploratory research because the dependent and independent variables are imprecisely defined by theory.
- *External validity* – the study uses multiple sites.
- *Reliability* – the study can relate the interview findings to prior surveys and studies.

The field-based research requires an interpretation of multiple realities which might lead to a loss of objectivity and validity (Scapens, 1990). The researchers tackled this issue by joint attendance at all but one of the interviews. Each researcher reviewed their independent notes of the interview against the transcription of the recording. All agreed interview reports were returned to interviewees to authenticate the accuracy of the interview.

The researchers were aware of the potential problems associated with researcher bias. This limitation was addressed at the outset by allowing the interviewees to choose the specific cross-border intra-group transaction for discussion and then position that transaction within its organisational and environmental context.

Time pressures limited the amount of involvement that each participant could devote to the study. The duration of the interviews ranged from about one to three hours, each interviewee received interview reports to comment on, follow-up telephone calls for necessary clarifications, and some participants communicated with further faxes or letters. Ideally, some follow-up interviews might have been preferable, but all the participants were senior managers with full diaries. We are therefore grateful for their valuable contributions.

Because of the diverse industries, the range of chosen specific cross-border intra-group transactions, and the small sample size, the findings cannot be generalised to a larger population. However, the researchers are not attempting to generalise, but more to specify under what circumstances certain relationships or insights identified in the study might hold. Our intention is to try to detect the issues underlying ITP for specific transactions, and, in particular, whether tangibles, intangibles and services merit different considerations.

The fieldwork therefore builds on the earlier survey. In respect to participants, i.e. their function and level of seniority and in terms of parent company nationality and activities, the fieldwork broadly reflects the survey. The size of company, the predominant type of international internal transaction, the significance of internal trade, the ITP methods used and the important influences on ITP are comparable between the fieldwork and survey samples. Nevertheless, we would not recommend that the fieldwork interviews are generalisable even for the survey companies in total. This is because specific individual transactions are the primary focus of the fieldwork, whereas the survey relates to the group transfer-pricing policy in general. There is no guarantee that these transactions are typical for the individual company. In the academic jargon, we are emphasising construct validity over reliability. The aim of this chapter is the more limited one of placing the characteristics of the field-based research participants in the context of the prior survey.

3

Global Commerciality

All twelve of the companies chose to describe individual transactions which to a lesser or greater extent reflected the view of operating in a global market. This chapter conveys the interconnected complexity of operations within MNEs and demonstrates the entanglement of ITP with royalty payments and other agreements or arrangements. For ease of presentation, the activities are divided into financial services, products and headquarter and other services, and then concludes with the relationship between ITP and royalties.

3.1 Financial services

All five of the MNEs chose to describe particular transactions which related to their main activity, i.e. the provision of financial services. Figure 3.1 indicates the complexity relating to a non-US-dollar swap derivatives transaction of Company 11.

Figure 3.1 Non-US-dollar swap derivative transactions
(——► flow of orders; --------► flow of fees)

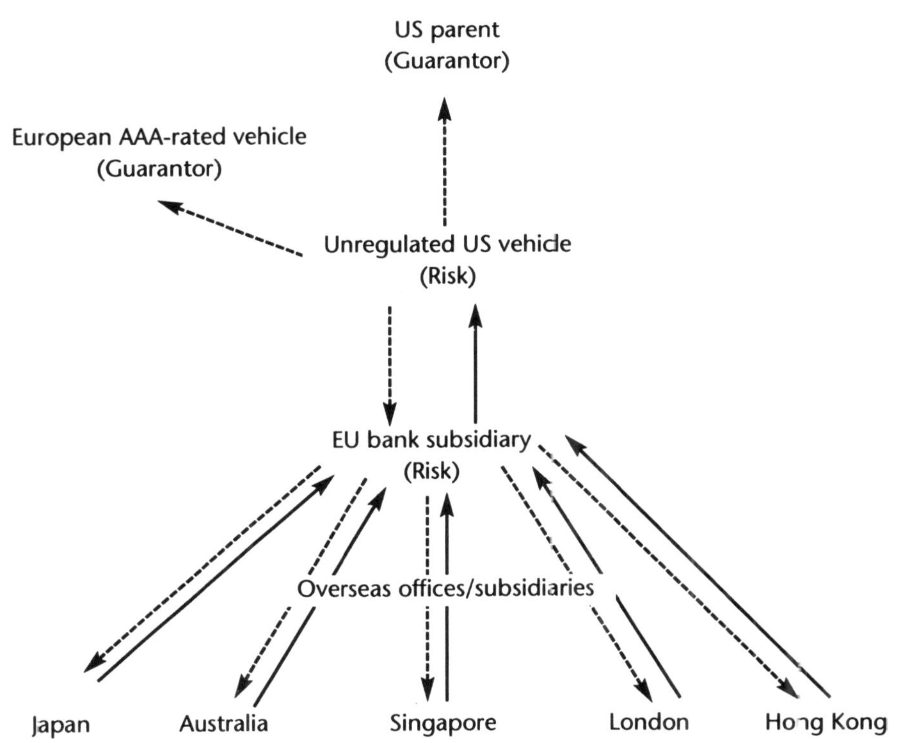

Transactions are generated by subsidiaries normally outside the USA which can use an Irish subsidiary as an intermediary or a non-EU vehicle such as the Swiss subsidiary to place business with the unregulated US vehicle. The AAA-rated Swiss subsidiary and the US parent act as guarantors for all swaps business. Thus, the major concerns are which subsidiaries or vehicles bear the credit-rating risk, where the capital is located and which subsidiaries generate or execute the transaction. These issues appear common to many transactions in financial services.

For example, when the purchase or sale of equities on the London Stock Exchange is undertaken by a UK subsidiary for clients generated by sister subsidiaries overseas, the generation and execution activities are performed by distinct parts of the same company (Company 5). In institutional investment management and corporate finance (Company 6), the same issue arises. Company 7 demonstrates a transaction in UK government stocks (gilts) where the client was originated by European, Asian or North American subsidiaries. In such cases, all the fee is identified in the UK but the overseas offices have incurred the costs of generating the clients. Without some form of transfer pricing, the overseas subsidiaries are inevitably loss-makers.

Some activities are truly worldwide markets, such as foreign exchange option trading where the responsibility for the global book is jointly held by several subsidiaries in any one 24-hour period. All the subsidiaries have traders, operations and back office support facilities which are virtually identical, and when the markets close in one part of the globe, the book and the risk management for the positions move to a sister subsidiary where the markets are open. When, as is the case in Company 8, all the trades use a single unregulated US entity, an ITP is essential to recognise the contribution each individual subsidiary has made.

Many of the participants returned to the theme that the financial services industry attempts to gain the maximum benefit by locating capital in appropriate regulated or unregulated entities. The location of capital and risk management is therefore determined on a global basis.

3.2 Products

Of the four MNEs whose primary activities are to supply products, three chose to describe a specific transaction relating to their primary business. Company 3 provided an example of the provision of freight services and is reported separately in section 6.4. All the specific transactions involve vertical integration of business operations across national boundaries. An example of the interconnectedness is offered by Company 1 and shown in Figure 3.2.

It was quickly realised that description of a single transaction failed to recognise the complex flows of knowledge and products. The full sequence of intra-group transactions consists of R&D, supply of raw materials, manufacture of proprietary intermediate product, manufacture of final product and, ultimately, distribution of the final product. In Company 1, final-product manufacturers concentrate on different ranges and, hence, there are high levels of cross-border transactions with manufacturers of a specific product supplying other manufacturers/distributors in the group. Even when

Figure 3.2: A vertically integrated transaction (numbers 1, 2 and 3 are illustrative of manufacturing and distributing units in Europe)

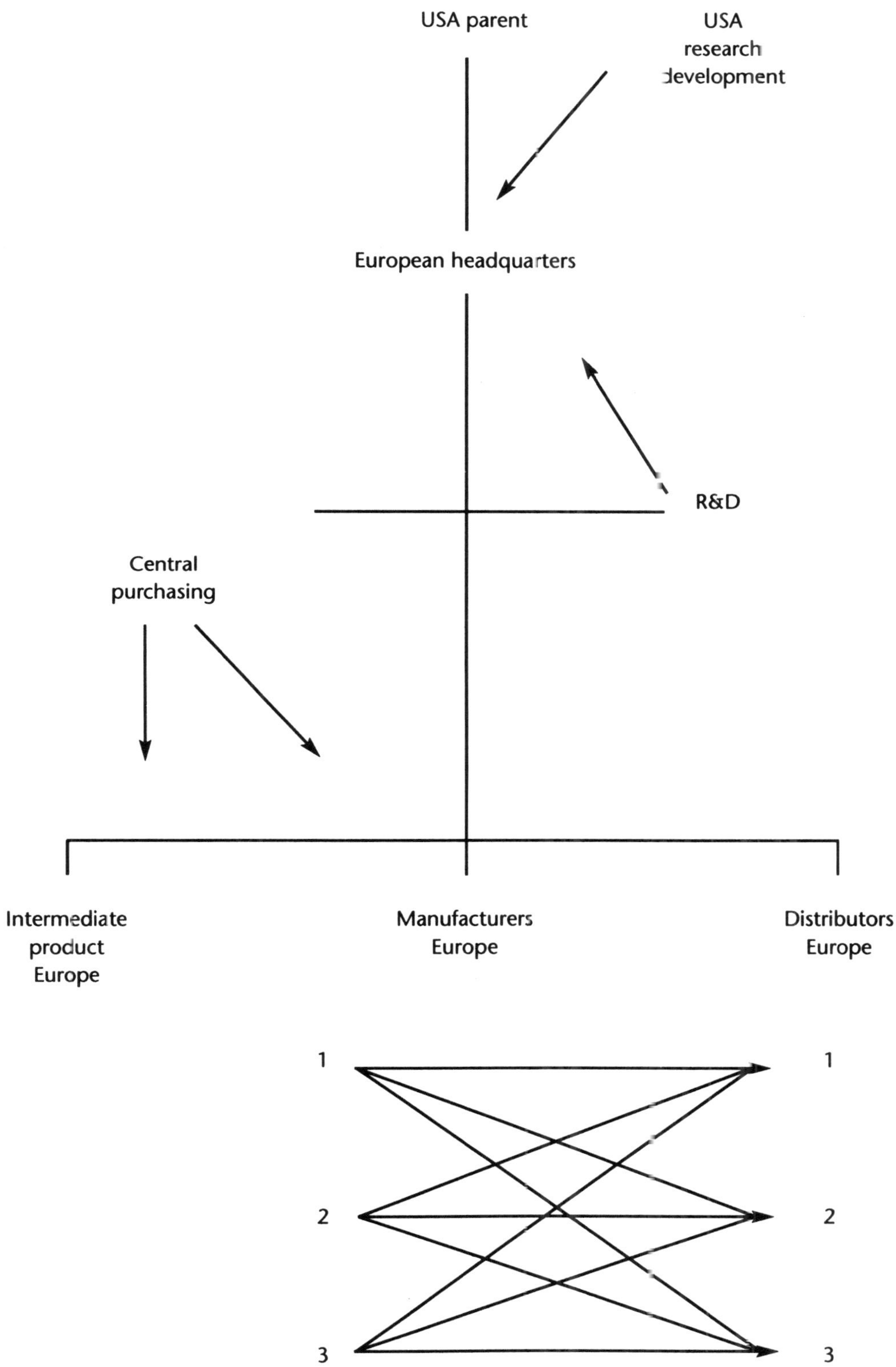

confined to the European operations, this results in a series of intra-group transactions reflecting the degree of interconnectedness of the business units. Considerations of economies of scale in the manufacture of intermediate and final product, and raw material purchase, explain the evolution of this pattern of flows. Investment in specific assets and the need for high utilisation rates appear to influence the location of business units.

Similar themes are evident in Company 2, where the final product is distinguished by different brands for different product markets. The parent is based in the UK and, of the 80 or more subsidiaries worldwide, four subsidiaries are 'brand-holders'. Technical, R&D, legal and taxation services are provided centrally. The UK parent contracts for the output of the brand-holder operating companies and then markets and sells on to subsidiaries in other parts of the world and to independent distributors. ITP covers the production of the final product and, in addition, a separate royalty paid to brand-holders on all sales made by the UK parent. Subsidiaries, other than brand-holders, may produce for their local markets and, to avoid undue competitiveness between local and international brands, the UK parent is responsible for marketing and setting prices of brand-holders' output in specific countries or regions. Also, the basic raw material for the final product is purchased centrally by the UK parent. Once more, the focus on a single transaction has necessitated recognition of a series of intra-group connections. The UK parent provides central services in addition to the purchase of the basic raw material; the brand-holder operating companies provide final product for the parent; the parent determines marketing and sales policy globally. Vertical integration appears to be enhanced by the fundamental involvement of the parent company, which is following a global marketing strategy.

Company 4 operates in a highly regulated global industry where the purchasers of final product are either government ministries or agents. Research and development is of critical importance to maintain a portfolio of new products. We focused on the manufacture and distribution of one new product. Inevitably, this led to the identification of a series of related intra-group transactions.

An R&D company creates intellectual property which is supplied to a UK group company. The latter grants licences to primary manufacturing companies in either the UK or the Far East which are part of the group. Secondary manufacturing companies provide the packaging, applicators, etc., for the primary manufacturing companies. All output is technically sold to a European clearing company, in the group which, in turn, sells to different markets worldwide via marketing subsidiaries. The European company has a commercial unit which facilitates agreement on ITP between the marketing subsidiaries and the European clearing company, the primary and secondary manufacturers and the European clearing company and the intellectual property company and the primary manufacturers. This elaborate series of intra-group transactions is justified by the highly regulated final-product market and the vast sums involved in R&D. The end result is that commercial reality requires a series of intra-group transactions to be examined, many of which inevitably cross national borders.

3.3 Services and headquarters services

Three of the MNEs participating in this fieldwork study chose services as the specific transaction. In the cases of Companies 10 and 12 this is consistent with their main activities, whereas for Company 9, the specific services transaction is related to, but distinct from, the main public relations or advertising operations. Several of the companies in the financial services and products section also referred to ITP relating to headquarter services.

Company 9 operates in the UK, the Americas, Continental Europe and Asia Pacific, with the head office located in the UK. Headquarters provides finance and marketing functions which are charged out to the regional subsidiaries. The intention is to recover cost and, currently, over 60 per cent of headquarters costs are charged out. Two reasons are offered for a cost ITP. First, the strength of sterling makes comparable local alternatives more attractive to overseas subsidiaries, and this would be magnified with the addition of a mark-up. Secondly, there is a perverse risk in charging out headquarters services on the basis of time spent when some overseas subsidiaries are loss-makers. When an overseas subsidiary is loss-making, more headquarters staff time is typically spent to achieve a turnaround. However, in the short term, the management charge-out costs increase for the subsidiary and, consequently, that subsidiary may need to be recapitalised or financed with additional loans from the UK. Hence, there is an interconnectedness between ITP policy and other decisions.

Company 10 focuses on the expertise provided by the UK subsidiary of a US parent. Expertise on platform engineering, exploration in specific locations and related advice is provided to sister subsidiaries and joint-venture partners. ITP is based on actual costs plus a mark-up, the budgets being adjusted to actuals at the year end. Costs are accumulated for the UK subsidiary's office and staff costs plus overheads and any allocation of costs from the US parent. These are converted to hourly rates for different staff functions, such as engineers, secretaries, accountants, etc. The hourly charge-out rate does not vary whether the services are provided intra-group or to joint-venture partners. While this does not give comparable uncontrolled prices, because each contract will require a different combination of personnel skills, the hourly rates can be justified ultimately by reference to time sheets and the cost-accumulation process. Subject to tax authority approval, the ITP of these service agreements seems uncontentious but, occasionally, payment may be offered as one month's oil production or 20 per cent of the oil produced where the equivalence with the normal cost-plus mark-up may be difficult to demonstrate. While other subsidiaries are able to obtain service agreements outside the group, the twin problems of guaranteeing the same level of expertise without endangering commercial confidentiality are likely to make this a rare occurrence. Perhaps owing to the specificity of the service required and the investment in human capital, Company 10 has limited the discretion of subsidiaries to enter into non-group transactions.

Our final participating company, Company 12, is long established in the provision of engineering services, and the parent is located in the USA. The specific transaction or series of transactions relate to the provision of engineering services by a newly created Indian subsidiary. Normal practice in this industry is to tender for contracts, and the business development unit in the USA is normally responsible for this cost-accumulation exercise. Owing to the relatively low cost of engineering services provision from the Indian subsidiary, this cost became the economic benchmark within the group and was incorporated in the tenders. Once obtained, the contract becomes the responsibility of a project manager who can decide, within the constraints of the budget, which subsidiaries will provide which services. The Indian subsidiary, however, did not achieve a level of activity commensurate with reporting a profit in either of its first two years of operation. Project managers appeared to be concerned about the perceived quality of work provided by the Indian subsidiary, but any increase in ITP would create a further disincentive for project managers to use that subsidiary. Effectively, intra-group transactions were being distorted by a low-cost, uniform ITP, with the potential implication that the tax authorities in India might justifiably enquire why losses continued to be reported. The company's solution was to use two ITPs (i.e. two sets of books). For internal purposes, the Indian subsidiary ITP was no longer uniform but complied with practices elsewhere in the group and varied with the project, industry, market and associated risk factors with a specific contract. Officially, and for tax-filing purposes, the ITP was increased in order that break-even and profit became feasible outcomes after the first two years of loss-making. This demonstrates the potential tension between the reasons for the strategic investment decision initially and the consequences of employing a compatible ITP. Again, the interconnectedness of decisions involving intra-group transactions is illustrated.

3.4 ITP and royalties

While several of the MNEs in the financial services, services and headquarters services sections alluded to their companies having ITPs relating to royalties, it was in those circumstances where the transaction was product-focused that royalty agreements commonly emerged. For Companies 1, 2 and 4, competitive advantage appears to be strongly linked with an effective and largely centralised R&D and/or purchasing function. The creation of intellectual property by the former function provides the basis for royalty payments by manufacturing subsidiaries operating overseas. The latter function results in management charges or fees being created.

In the case of Company 1, royalties are subject to an ITP based on all third-party sales by the operating subsidiaries. This means that the manufacturing/distributing subsidiary's performance is influenced by two forms of ITP, one relating to the physical flow of product and the second to intellectual property or R&D. Similarly, in Company 2, royalties are paid by the UK parent to the brand-holder subsidiaries for product development of international brands. For central R&D and purchasing, payments from all subsidiaries, including the brand-holders, are covered by royalty agreements. Likewise, in Company 4, manufacturing subsidiaries pay royalties in respect of the licences obtained from the UK company which commercially develops the intellectual property of central R&D. Again, at least one stage in the production process is subject to two ITPs – in this instance, the ITP at which the manufacturer's output flows to the European clearing company and the ITP delivering royalties to the R&D commercial subsidiary.

Informed readers may not be surprised by this close association between product flows and royalty payments. Such knowledge-based payments may be expected to explain the MNEs' competitive advantage in a global market. The recognition that, not only in products but in financial services, services and headquarters services, cross-border transactions are common and connected appears evident from the fieldwork. The additional recognition that royalty and product ITPs appear conterminously indicates a further necessary expansion of the analysis for this form of transaction. If the fieldwork participants are typical, it is obvious that ITP cannot be defined by a single transaction. Vertical integration, interconnected decisions and sequential interdependence changes in corporate structure and changes in regulatory requirements need to be identified in order that sense can be made of ITP which reflects global commerciality. None of the twelve participants provided evidence of ITP relating to trademarks or names, but this may not mean that they do not occur.

4

Corporate Strategy

The relationship between corporate strategy and transfer pricing is potentially complex. One view is that strategy determines the pricing policy and thus offers the opportunity to guarantee the success of the strategy. An alternative and opposite perspective suggests that the need for the pricing policy to be responsive to dynamic market changes necessitates an ongoing reappraisal of strategy (Elliott, 1999). Fieldwork based on twelve companies is not capable of providing a definitive answer to the direction of this relationship, but insights may be offered to detect influential factors in specific situations. These factors may include the way in which the company is structured, the use of external advisers, the basis of providing rewards and the nature of the global industry. We begin the analysis by examining the degree of regulation in the global markets faced by the twelve participating MNEs.

4.1 Regulated environments

Of all the participating companies, it is those in the financial services industry which perceive the link between strategy, ITP and regulated environment as most pronounced. The underlying message is that these MNEs are 'very sensitive on capital and try to use it as effectively as possible' (Company 8). Regulations obviously differ by countries and the nature of the specific transaction. Unregulated entities may be used for non-US-dollar swap derivatives in the USA if appropriate guarantors are available (Company 11). As subsidiaries or affiliates improve their credit-rating positions, the location for providing capital and guarantees changes, thereby creating new intra-group relationships. Company 11, for example, explained that unregulated entities in the USA are not permitted to trade in bonds and, for this reason, the equity derivatives activity moved to a regulated UK entity.

This concern with strategic management of capital is also illustrated by Company 8, where non-US-dollar swaps are risk-managed and traded in London, but all transactions are booked on to a US unregulated entity in the group. The vast majority of personnel are located in the UK, the US parent provides guarantees and the unregulated US entity assumes the credit and market risk. In financial services it therefore appears that the strategic location of capital relative to the different regulations in different countries governs the subsequent intra-group transactions.

Other examples of regulations having an influence over the location of subsidiaries relate to the ability to trade. A regulated individual is required as part of an Italian legal entity to sell swaps in that country.

One of the service-providing MNEs (Company 12) indicated that the foreign direct investment (FDI) decision is influenced by the availability of indigenous, quality personnel and the proximity to emerging markets. However, regulations in India do not allow the creation of branches and, at the time, the parent was not prepared to make an equity investment when repatriation of equity was virtually impossible and foreign exchange restrictions made dividend distributions very difficult. Eventually, an investment by means of loan capital was agreed with the host government and the subsidiary established.

Several companies across the sample indicated that, after the FDI is made, it was of equal importance to avoid locating profits in high-tax jurisdictions as it was to record losses in countries when no tax relief is available. Making full use of the loss carry-over regulations in the different jurisdictions may not be an influence on the initial strategic investment, but they appear to be of some significance once the intra-group trade becomes operational.

4.2 Internal structures

The structures within the MNE which govern intra-group transactions seems more idiosyncratic where product transfers are involved. Central purchasing units within the parent company appear to be common. Centralised (and some regional) R&D units are also common. Decisions about the location of primary and secondary manufacturers obviously influence product transfers.

Company 2 also explained how a change in strategy resulted in more involvement in intra-group transactions by the parent. The previous strategy allowed subsidiaries, particularly brand-holders, to compete in the same geographic market. The change to targeting specific brands to specific markets results in the parent becoming more responsible for technical, R&D, legal and taxation services. The flow of transactions also changed in that now all subsidiaries' output is technically bought by the parent, which deals with sister subsidiaries and independent distributors for the ultimate sale of output.

The need for company-specific structures appears most necessary when product MNEs face highly regulated environments. Company 4, for example, has created an intermediary company to manage intellectual property, a European clearing company which is essentially a re-invoicing operation, and a commercial team which sets and adjudicates ITP. The commercial team is needed to facilitate changes in ITP between all subsidiaries in the production process and reviews transfer prices quarterly. As the ultimate sale of output is to government ministries or agents, unexpected events can occur, as in Japan where a new regulation required all prices to be reduced by 8 or 9 per cent. In this specific instance, the personnel of the commercial team are a unit distinct from the internal tax department or finance function, and their function is to facilitate the necessary adjustments to the ITP policy in order to minimise the disruption resulting from such an unexpected event.

The financial services and service providers we interviewed do not appear to need special internal structures to govern intra-group relationships. However, regardless of the form of transaction or the main business of the MNE, each parent and several of the major subsidiaries employ internal tax specialists.

4.3 Internal advisers

All our interviews were conducted with tax directors or tax managers of the parent company or UK subsidiary. The size of the internal tax departments not surprisingly varied, with the participant representing a parent or subsidiary company. For example, Company 11 in financial services has a complement of nineteen tax professionals, two of whom are transfer-pricing specialists responsible for about 60–90 internal agreements. Company 8, which is also a UK financial services subsidiary of a US parent, has approximately 70 specialists in its tax department. Dependent on whether a review or fiscal audit is under way, some senior tax personnel may be spending about 25–33 per cent of their time on ITP.

At the other end of the spectrum, one of the service-provision MNEs devotes 5 per cent of the internal tax department's time to ITP. This is the UK subsidiary of a US parent (Company 10). A UK parent in the service-provision industry has one tax professional who deals with all matters relating to transfer pricing (Company 9).

Company 4, a product manufacturer, has seven tax professionals at the UK parent who are estimated to spend 50 per cent of their time on ITP issues. Company 2 indicated that there was an internal tax department of some significant size at the UK parent location. There are literally hundreds of internal agreements relating to the flows of tangibles and intangibles which include technical and advisory, R&D, central purchasing, royalty agreements (regarding trademarks and brands) and, inevitably, end-product transfer agreements. These agreements involve subsidiary managers, parent company tax specialists, trademark lawyers and senior finance personnel.

Several of the participating MNEs indicated that, when dealing with the tax authorities of jurisdictions overseas, local advisers, normally accounting practitioners, act on behalf of the subsidiary. An enquiry by the host fiscal authority concerning ITP normally results in the parent tax department being called in.

One interesting development which appears at this time to be confined to the US parent MNEs in financial services is the use of specialist law firms. Effectively, these firms verify that an arm's-length transfer price is being used. This provides, in this instance Company 11, a capability to sue the law firm should the ITP not be deemed acceptable by the fiscal authorities. There is also some evidence of specialist law firms in the USA managing the advance pricing agreement (APA) process and economists providing advice on functional analysis (Company 8). Chapter 5 explores these issues in greater depth.

4.4 Reward schemes

Certainly in the literature on domestic transfer pricing, the potential of rewards linked to business-unit performance to cause unintended managerial behaviour is fully recognised (Drury, 1996; Merchant 1998). This does not appear to apply to ITP in all twelve of the MNEs in this study.

4.4.1 In financial services

For all these companies, the association between annual manager or trader bonus and the financial performance of their specific subsidiaries is, at best, tenuous. A primary explanation is that the markets which these MNEs serve are perceived as global. Company 7 illuminated the situation by describing the management accounts as based on global products. The different lines of business (swaps, gilts, etc.) are recognised as having different fee structures. In fact, certain products have attractive fee structures set centrally to incentivise traders to push particular products. This alerts traders to concentrate on particular products. The parent company is therefore able to evaluate global profitability by lines of business, and the chief executive will determine the bonus for the main subsidiaries by reference to the total group performance. Each subsidiary has discretion as to how the allocated bonus is divided between products and regions. In this, local market conditions prevail and traders are rewarded subjectively, one consideration being their attractiveness to competitor firms and whether a bonus will influence staff retention or not. This view is repeated and confirmed, for example by Company 6 which states that even if a business is loss-making, the bonus is still paid to stop the key players going elsewhere.

Similar conditions appear to apply to those employees responsible for building client relationships. The expertise of these generators of business may border on the unique, and retention of their services is therefore of importance (Company 8).

4.4.2 In products

For the three manufacturing MNEs, the link between managerial rewards and financial performance of the subsidiaries appears strong. Some form of budgeted profit is employed in all three companies, and this incorporates ITP. Additionally, repatriated cash to the parent is an important reward-triggering mechanism in Companies 1 and 2. For Company 4, the marketing subsidiaries' capability to reach and exceed sales targets influences reward payments. At this level of analysis, ITP may be perceived by some subsidiary managers as conflict-generating, which may result in gaming and time-consuming arbitration. Company 4 already appears to have recognised this by the establishment of a commercial team to facilitate ITP adjustments and to negotiate these with the European clearing company. Company 2 also recognises the dangers of linking rewards to subsidiary financial performance.

This MNE has experience of ITP which may be tax advantageous for the group but adversely affects a subsidiary's performance. On these occasions, the internal tax department acts as arbiter. To handle the adverse effect, a distinction can be made between performance indicators reflecting managerial as opposed to the subsidiary's effectiveness. Also, when the group benefit reduces a manager's performance measure, a profit-relief system operates to demonstrate the reason for apparent under-achievement.

The impression of profit-centre management tying managerial rewards to subsidiary financial performance is more strongly given than in the financial service MNEs. Nevertheless, mechanisms appear to be in place to mitigate the worst effects associated with centrally administered ITP.

4.4.3 Services and headquarters services

Company 9, where headquarters costs associated with the finance and marketing functions are charged out to overseas subsidiaries, also distinguishes performance measurement of the manager and the subsidiary. Managers are evaluated on operating profit, revenues less operating costs, with management charges appearing below the line unless they are directly attributable.

The management of the UK subsidiary which provides services for the upstream oil business (Company 10) is rewarded on the financial performance of the region to which it belongs. It is argued that aggregation of results to regions reduces the ITP impact and does not adversely affect an individual subsidiary manager's ability to be rewarded.

The situation in Company 12 is more complex, possibly because of the use of a matrix organisation structure. Project managers are evaluated on a measure of profit after indirect but before direct taxation. In addition, the subsidiary management providing the engineering services in different locations, including India, are evaluated and rewarded.

The measure of performance draws project managers' attention to customs duties but not income tax. The internal tax department sometimes persuaded project managers to take actions which minimised income taxes even if extra indirect taxes resulted. Consensus is aided by the project managers' bonus being based on group after-tax profit. Greater acceptance of profit after all taxes as a relevant measure by project managers is reinforced by the reward scheme.

For the subsidiary manager in India, the use of two sets of accounts to record different ITPs meant that this was a special case. Given the strategy adopted by Company 12 to use India as the economic benchmark internally, the use of financial performance indicators is replaced by targets to attain break-even and to meet utilisation rates. The latter may be of critical importance in gaining acceptance of the quality of the Indian subsidiary's services within the group.

4.5 Exceptions

The choice of the cross-border transactions described related in almost all cases to the main activities of the individual participating MNEs. Where this is not the case, the impression is given of a different form of ITP being employed; for example, Company 3 appeared to use a whole variety of transfer-pricing methods – even varying year on year for the same services. There is no legitimate reason why an MNE may not use different ITPs for different forms of transaction. The number of internal agreements which appear to exist (Companies 2 and 11) seem to reflect this. This study addresses only one or a series of related intra-group transactions, and therefore any influences even about one MNE's ITP practices must be treated with caution.

In fact, several of the MNEs indicated when there are exceptions to the ITP situation being described. For example, subsidiaries which are in a start-up situation or are not able to offer a full range of services comparable with sister subsidiaries are subject to different methods of transfer pricing (Companies 1 and 6).

In specific situations, an offshore company may be created in order to receive and blend dividends from subsidiaries experiencing a range of quite different host country income tax rates. The aim is to maximise the use of tax credits and to avoid the wastage of much foreign tax credit, as when a subsidiary is subject to, say, 50 per cent income tax rates.

Likewise, several of the MNEs reported that normal ITP methods and processes are adjusted when specific transactions involve subsidiaries in locations where tax holidays or special tax deals apply, or in developing countries with evolving or more restrictive tax systems.

This is certainly not a comprehensive list of the occasions when, or reasons why, there are exceptions to the 'normal' ITP policy. For companies of this size and complexity, the task to record all the exceptions would display Herculean proportions, given the dynamics of global markets. Yet this may need to be addressed if the justification of ITP under self-assessment is to be successful.

4.6 Conclusions

All twelve participating MNEs indicate a strong central management involvement in ITP. This may not necessarily result in the price being set centrally, although there is some evidence of this, but certainly the process and mechanism by which ITP is applied and adjusted are subject to central management control. This may be a direct result of following global strategies, for in each transaction the need to co-ordinate the activities of more than one subsidiary to deliver goods or services to the client is obvious. The degree of regulation in different environments also influences the form of the intra-group transactions, sometimes profoundly, as in the case of financial services and pharmaceuticals. In some other companies or industries, ITP is long established and stable, meaning that there would have to be a very good reason for justifying a change to the existing system.

The commercial reality of operating in global markets appears most complex when products are the focus of the intra-group trade. A series of interconnected transactions occur which include two forms of ITP. One relates to the tangible product flows, while the other relates to intangible and royalty payments.

The significance of ITP is perhaps reflected in the number of internal agreements displayed by some of the MNEs and the commitment to the internal tax function. The role of these specialists to render ITP tax-effective and justifiable and to monitor, if not liaise with, fiscal authorities over enquiries or reviews enables central management to delegate the day-to-day operation of the ITP process. Increasing use of the expertise of external economists and lawyers is apparent in a minority of the participating MNEs. Compliance costs may therefore expand in future, with the additional complications inherent in product transfers fuelling these further.

The intricacies of the product flows and royalty payments, both of which can influence the financial performance of a single subsidiary, have led some MNEs to introduce or include as part of the ITP mechanism conflict-resolution measures. Some companies distinguish performance measures for the subsidiary and the manager.

Elsewhere, an internal team to arbitrate or mediate ITP is observed. These steps appear to be necessary to maintain the motivation of subsidiary managers associated with rewards linked to some form of profit, cash flow and/or sales growth measures.

In this respect, practices in the financial services sector appear relatively straightforward. Managerial reward is effectively decoupled from subsidiary measures of financial performance. Central management is concerned with the global performance of different services, most of which require co-operation between managers of traders located in different parts of the world. Reward is fundamentally judgemental at many different levels of the hierarchy. This may prove difficult to justify under a functional analysis (see Chapter 5).

For those MNEs providing non-financial services, judicious use of basing rewards on group or regional performance is observed. Any distortion due to ITP is thereby avoided, although the award of incentive payments subsequently to more disaggregated units of the business may be contentious.

It should be noted that these observations of apparent differences and similarities are open to an alternative interpretation. While we have attempted to analyse the transaction chosen by the participating MNEs, we are also aware that exceptions occur: for example, when a subsidiary is being established or does not yet offer a full range of services. Also, these transactions and their corporate context are described at a single point in time. We have emphasised that the transfer-pricing policies are under continued review and subject to changes based on a host of different factors (e.g. corporate structure; regulatory requirements; reviews required by fiscal authorities).

5

Fiscal Relationships

This chapter considers the nature of the relationships that exist between the MNEs and fiscal authorities around the world. All twelve MNEs have experience of either fiscal enquiries or audits from at least one fiscal authority concerning their international transfer pricing. There appear to be both formal and informal relationships, ranging from a historical 'understanding' at one end of the spectrum to an advance pricing agreement (APA) at the other. Indeed, some of the MNEs demonstrate very well-established relationships with fiscal authorities. The majority of these relationships relate to either the Inland Revenue (in the UK) or the IRS (in the USA). In addition, several changes in relationships have emerged during the course of the field study.

5.1 Formal and informal relationships

In the more regulated industries there appears to be a much closer relationship between the MNEs and the fiscal authorities. In the UK, the Oil Taxation Office (OTO) is a special section of the International Division of the Inland Revenue which deals exclusively with oil companies and maintains a database on all those companies. This specialisation means that the OTO possesses a good understanding of the industry and the nature of oil companies' intra-group transactions. Company 3 receives transfer-pricing enquiries every year from the OTO, so it now voluntarily provides the OTO with listings of all its intra-group transactions on an annual basis. Company 10 acknowledges that it has a well-established relationship with the OTO and that this relationship enables informal clearances to be offered and agreed in advance of the service agreements becoming operational. In fact, Company 10 argues in favour of the approach of the OTO ('I think the OTO likes to be seen to be commercial. If you go in with a commercial argument, they will normally follow it up') and the general role that they play ('... the OTO appears to be working quite effectively as a collector but also as an adviser to the industry. Maybe the International Division should think about setting up one (equivalent to OTO) for financial services, etc.'). Contrast this with Company 3's view that 'a more realistic and commercial approach by the IR' is a primary requirement.

In the USA, Company 4 (in the pharmaceutical industry) sends annually to the IRS a 'statement of fact' listing all inter-affiliate transactions. Furthermore, there is a likelihood that, as fiscal authorities increase their networking, similar 'statements' might need to be provided to show to other fiscal authorities. This may be to the benefit of all parties, especially if the competent authority procedures can be improved by increased transparency and/or expediency.

Other companies/industries also demonstrate long-standing relationships with the IRS. Company 12 (in the engineering services industry) has developed a well-established relationship with the IRS over the last 40 years, consistent with most large US companies, and an IRS representative has a permanent room at its headquarters in the USA. Under this relationship, reviews and liaisons have therefore been commonplace. Similarly, financial services Company 8 acknowledges a well-established relationship with the IRS and a closer understanding with the Inland Revenue. This group handles most tax enquiries centrally, but there are also tax specialists at each of the main subsidiaries who can deal with local inspectors overseas. In the UK, Company 9 (in the advertising industry) has a satisfactory 'arrangement' with the Inland Revenue – in the form of verbal assurances from the Inland Revenue covering the next two or three years.

The picture is undoubtedly partial, but it seems that large companies in regulated industries have interacted with UK and US fiscal agents on a semi-formal basis. The level of interaction is enhanced also by increased mobility of tax inspectors joining MNEs.

5.2 Documentation

A number of themes emerge regarding levels of supporting documentation.

Good documentation

Linked to the well-established relationships with the OTO, Company 10 stressed that trust (and therefore the availability of advance clearances) is built and reinforced over time by having detailed records and clear processes to uphold the computation of transfer prices.

The influence of the IRS

It is evident that the IRS has set the benchmarks for international transfer pricing and documentation requirements. Companies 2, 5, 8 and 9 (which have US parent companies) have all implemented policies to comply with US requirements. In particular, Companies 2 and 8 have used functional analysis and Company 5 has used CPM to implement group policy because the IRS has accepted this approach. In relation to documentation, Company 2 has adopted the IRS regulations on document retention as group policy for all subsidiaries ('This is the policy that we follow for US purposes and we feel that this will be good enough anywhere else'), and Company 9 has had to respond to tax authorities' enquiries about the documentation of management charges ('The group operates on the basis that if the Inland Revenue and the IRS can be satisfied, then a comparable level of documentation should be adequate for overseas tax jurisdictions').

Onerous requirements

Companies 1, 4 and 9 stated that the documentation requirements are onerous. Company 4 reported that both documentation and compliance costs are increasing, but that after the initial compliance costs are met, it would not be too expensive to maintain documentation. Company 1 has been subject to an Inland Revenue enquiry, and the documentation and compliance costs associated with this enquiry were extremely onerous, particularly having to document both purchases and sales for both internal and external transactions. Company 9 is very critical of the demands of documentation:

> I suppose the biggest bugbear is going to be the answer you will get from a lot of people, i.e. the amount of documentation that you have to keep. I think that once you have a policy which is acceptable to the local revenue authority, we would like to say we can use the same methodology on a worldwide basis and replicate the documentation. The provision of different documentation for different authorities is extremely time-consuming.

Furthermore, 'I spend an awful lot of time doing transfer-pricing documentation and it is not a value-adding exercise at all.'

5.3 APAs

As discussed in section 5.1, some groups have verbal assurances or existing relationships with fiscal authorities and therefore do not consider that APAs are necessary. In contrast, three of the financial service groups are very interested in arranging APAs but have met with varying degrees of success.

Companies not interested in APAs

These groups already have the levels of assurance regarding transfer-pricing policies that they require. Companies 2 and 3 have not contemplated entering an APA, with Company 3 viewing it as 'time-consuming and it is arguing before the event'; Company 5 has just implemented a new policy and does not consider that further changes (i.e. an APA) are warranted at the moment, though the possibility of an APA is not totally excluded; Company 9 considers that the costs of an APA exceed the benefits; Company 12 perceives the need for an APA as minimal.

Companies interested in APAs

Company 7 has successfully renegotiated a bilateral APA (between the UK and the USA) for swaps a number of times since the early 1990s. Despite their success, the tax manager was pragmatic about the APA ('essentially the APA is a calculation done for tax and that's it') and emphasised that it is a difficult process. The APA is a bilateral (rather than multilateral) agreement because it was hard enough to satisfy the two authorities : 'So the APA process is not one to be recommended. It is one to be recommended in terms of getting certainty if the numbers are big enough' or the area is complex enough. Part of the difficulty is the way in which the APA process is conducted. In this company's past experience, any number from nine to eighteen IRS representatives have attended APA meetings. Often these IRS representatives do not appear to have discussed the case beforehand to agree a common agenda. Overall, the company must be satisfied with APAs because it is considering a possible bilateral agreement between the UK and Japan.

Company 8 has made a formal submission for a bilateral APA (between the UK and the USA) for non-US-dollar swaps to cover the period 1994–8. However, 'the submission was to cover 1994–8 so, you know, we are still miles apart with six months to go, so whether it's true to call it an advance pricing agreement is a matter of viewpoint'. If or when agreement is reached, it is the company's hope that the APA will apply for similar transactions prior to 1994 and for at least three years after 1998. The time consumed by high-ranking management and external advisers created significant costs. If the way the company is organised and the transaction dealt with has not changed, the need for a new APA seems unwarranted.

Despite the fact that the group has encountered a particularly difficult case with their APA submission and they are still negotiating, they also argue that this does not detract from the potential benefits of having APAs. Their ultimate wish would be for a quick APA procedure, but experience in other US companies suggests that it requires 1½–3 years to obtain an APA and the system has then generally worked satisfactorily.

Company 11 attempted to enter into a bilateral APA with the USA but it aborted this attempt and appears to be disillusioned with the process. The group entered into the APA process with the IRS but pulled out after 9–15 months of negotiations. The issue was not complex or difficult, but the group typically faced over twenty members of the IRS as part of the negotiation process.

5.4 Inland Revenue trends

Several trends emerge from the interviews concerning the direction of the Inland Revenue in terms of transfer pricing. One of the trends that accompanies the new UK transfer-pricing rules is that it is likely to be the local tax inspectors in the first instance who enquire about transfer-pricing matters. International Division is likely to be the technical back-up for smaller cases and will perhaps take the lead for larger cases. It is suggested that the Inland Revenue will concentrate particularly on those companies with limited documentation (i.e. the 'riskier' companies) for the next 5–10 years (Company 7).

Another feature of increased globalisation are the increased levels of communication between different tax authorities. Company 4 observes that 'authorities talk to each other' and this means that there is increased global transparency. Company 4 also emphasises that 'certainty is key' – anything that increases the level of certainty reduces the danger of different tax authorities all attacking a company. Similarly, Company 8 notes that the competent authorities under the double taxation treaty (for the IRS and the Inland Revenue) hold regular quarterly meetings where transfer- pricing issues can be discussed. However, the current competent authority procedure has received criticism for being a protracted process that needs improving (especially as there is likely to be a '10/20-fold increase in cross-border transactions' (Company 4)).

6

Transfer-pricing Methods in Practice

A number of patterns emerge in the transfer-pricing methods (TPMs) used across the twelve MNEs. In particular, some distinctions can be made between the TPMs appropriate for financial services versus products versus headquarters services.

6.1 TPMs in financial services

Profit-based methods

For the five financial services companies interviewed, some form of profit split appears to be the standard way for pricing intra-group transactions. More specifically, profit split is used for institutional investment management and corporate finance (Company 6), swaps (Company 7), advisory services and global banking (Company 8) and non-dollar swaps derivatives (Company 11). As discussed in Chapter 5, in some cases these TPMs have been agreed formally with the fiscal authorities (APA for Company 7; APA under negotiation for Company 8) and in some cases they have been agreed informally (e.g. Company 11 with the Inland Revenue).

Within a global financial services company, one of the main transfer-pricing issues relates to fee-splitting (Companies 5, 6, 7, 8 and 11). How should the fee be divided between that part of the group that generates the business/introduces the client and that part of the group that executes the work? In addition to splitting fees between generators and executors, a number of participants stressed the importance of rewarding different parts of the group for the location of risk and the location of capital (Companies 7, 8 and 11 discussed this in relation to swaps). There is often tension between companies and fiscal authorities about how risk and capital should be rewarded.

The starting position for fee-splitting between generators and executors varies, depending on the nature of the business. For instance, the generator might receive 75 per cent of the fee for institutional investment management where there is an ongoing relationship with the client (e.g. Company 6), but for corporate finance activities the generator might receive only 25 per cent of the fee (e.g. Company 6). In many corporate finance deals, the generator might also execute a portion of the business, in which case the fee might be split 50/50 between generator and executor. These discrete 25 per cent increments in the fee-splitting structure are also evident for Company 8's advisory services.

The IRS has accepted a profit-split method as appropriate for Company 8's global trading activities. In this instance, three factors are used to apply the profit-split method:

- expertise of the traders as measured by their relative compensation in each subsidiary;
- where the risk is borne, which is the USA in this case because all transactions are booked there;
- which subsidiaries provide operations or back-office functions to the trade as measured by the relative salary costs in each subsidiary.

To determine the profit split, the traders' expertise has a weighting of four, with the other factors having a weighting of one each. This displays the importance of the traders and allows a composite measure of each subsidiary's contribution to be measured.

Company 5 focused on equities management broking (the purchase and sale of equities worldwide on behalf of institutional investors), and since 1995 the comparable profits method (CPM) is the group's preferred transfer pricing policy. The initial motivation came from the USA where the IRS accepted this method. CPM is interpreted as:

> So if we had a company in this particular part of the world that was using a third party to transact business, what relative profit margins would they be making on that style of business, given the data that was available?

Transaction-based methods

Although profit-based methods appear to be more commonly applied TPMs to financial services, there is evidence that cost-based methods are used in some circumstances. Often, a group will run its small-scale established subsidiaries or start-up businesses (which are expected to make a loss in early years) on a cost-plus basis to begin with to avoid building up losses (Companies 6 and 7). This means that in the initial stages their costs determine their income. Once they start to generate sufficient income, they move from cost-plus to fee-splitting. Also, for instance, Company 7 has an agreed bilateral profit-split APA (between the UK and the USA), but because the German fiscal authority has not been keen to negotiate an APA, a cost plus 10 per cent policy is used in Germany. In addition to its group policy of CPM, Company 5 maintains documentary evidence of the full cost-plus process in order that fiscal challenges can be met.

6.2 TPMs for products

For main product transfers, Companies 1, 2 and 4 were the three specific cross-border intra-group transactions involving products. Although each of these examples used a transaction-based method for the main transaction, it was essential to have an understanding of the group corporate structure because there were other agreements in place. For instance, all three companies had royalty agreements in force: for R&D (Company 1), marketing (Company 2) and manufacturing licences (Company 4).

Companies 1 and 2 use full cost-plus for transfers of auto components and tobacco respectively, and Company 4 uses resale price methods for pharmaceutical products. Company 1 uses a simple, standard, fixed rate that applies to all products (cost plus 5 per cent) and it has been stable at this rate for many years. The rationale to support the policy is that if the global return on the product is 10 per cent, then it is reasonable to share that between the manufacturer and the distributor. This policy is effectively 'set in stone' and there are no plans to review or change it. Company 2 restructured three years ago for strategic marketing reasons, and the UK group contracts for production at a transfer price of standard cost plus 10 per cent.

Company 4 applies resale-minus because it is the most appropriate TPM for pharmaceutical products for a number of reasons:

- nearly every market in the world is regulated, which means that the host regulatory bodies often fix the final selling price – this is why profit split is not used;
- there are different prices appropriate to each market;
- the cost of manufacture is a very small proportion of the value of the final product – this is why cost-plus is not used.

6.3 TPMs for headquarters services

Three of the companies selected service provision as the specific cross-border intra-group transaction to discuss. In addition, a number of other companies mentioned their treatment of central services during the course of the interview. The three examples of service provision were for headquarters management services (Company 9), oil exploration services/advice (Company 10) and engineering services (Company 12). In general, the participants use transfer prices to charge out fully absorbed costs on a cost-only basis, but if these services are value-adding services then there is fiscal pressure to include a mark-up. In addition, it is not permitted to charge out the shareholder costs, which must remain with the plc.

Service provision at cost

Company 9 aims to recharge as much of head office costs as possible (and manages to charge out in excess of 60 per cent). This is partly tax-driven because of the UK's relatively low corporate income tax rate, but it is also an efficient way of remitting funds back to the UK. These functions are charged out at cost because the amount of value added attributable to these services is limited because of their nature (e.g. financial services; general management services). Following lengthy discussions, the Inland Revenue has accepted that these services can be recharged at cost (the Inland Revenue would naturally prefer a mark-up) as long as any marketing services or referrals, which do add value, are charged out with a mark-up.

Other participants discussed the transfer-pricing treatment of central costs or technical and advisory services. Company 2 charges out its technical services at cost based on a breakdown of time spent working for subsidiaries, and this procedure has been audited and agreed by the Inland Revenue. Company 7 allocates its central management costs (e.g. central finance; human resources; corporate communications) on a head-count basis (as does Company 6) or square-footage basis to the subsidiaries.

Very often these cost allocations are viewed as unfair by the subsidiaries. For instance, low-margin affiliated businesses (e.g. a photocopier leasing business) might object to apportionment based on head count (Company 6); central costs are often incurred working on a subsidiary but not at the request of that subsidiary manager (Company 2); sometimes subsidiaries do not appreciate the extent of the work or the real cost of the functions carried out by the head office (Company 9).

Finally, if overseas subsidiaries are running at a loss, the head office might try to minimise the charges to these countries because if they continue to pay management charges they might have to be recapitalised or financed with additional loans from the UK. To compound the problem, these subsidiaries are more likely to need to receive greater attention and time from head office staff (Company 9).

Service provision at cost plus a mark-up

Company 9 charges a 12.5 per cent mark-up on its value-adding services such as marketing services or referrals. One problem is that there are no available comparables or industry comparables, so this mark-up is agreed between the company and the Inland Revenue and reviewed every two or three years.

Company 10 provides expertise on platform engineering, exploration in specific locations, and related issues to order, for the group and joint ventures. Service agreements incorporate transfer prices which are based on actual cost (budgeted figures are adjusted to actual at the year end) plus a mark-up. The process of cost accumulation involves identification of the UK subsidiary's office and staff costs and overheads, plus any allocation of costs from the US parent. These costs are converted into hourly rates for different staff departments at the UK subsidiary. Considerable care is taken in this process because joint-venture partners are billed in the same way. Hence, for secretaries, engineers, accountants, etc., there will be an hourly rate for charge-out purposes. Overheads are allocated on traditional methods rather than ABC (activity-based costing). The potentially contentious issue concerns the mark-up or profit element which is added to the service agreement, but the mark-up is supported by documentation, comparables (with joint-venture partners) and informal agreement from the OTO.

Company 11 sets the transfer price of engineering services provided by an Indian subsidiary at a level (a single charge-out rate) which would have created a loss for the first two years of the start-up and then gradually to show a profit in years 3 and 4. After two years of losses, it became apparent that, from a tax viewpoint, they needed to increase the transfer price to enable the subsidiary to show profits. However, any increase in the price charged by the Indian subsidiary would create further disincentive to project managers to use the Indian operation. The group therefore set up two sets of books to handle the transfer pricing of engineering services. The transfer-pricing rate was increased for local and taxation reporting in order that a positive turnaround situation could be shown in the latter half of year 3. The group therefore issued, officially, invoices for the engineering services of India which formed part of the local tax reporting, but different transfer prices for the internal management report.

6.4 Negotiation: an unacceptable method

Company 3 focused on freight services to demonstrate the difficulties of applying the comparable uncontrolled price (CUP) method and to demonstrate that non-acceptance of negotiated transfer prices by fiscal authorities is inconsistent with decentralisation and profit-centre management. Taking the first of these points, Company 3 believed that an independent quote for freight services represented 'convincing and compelling evidence' of a CUP on which they based their own transfer price. However, the Inland Revenue questioned whether the CUP was correctly adjusted and an investigation is currently under way. In relation to the second point, negotiated transfer prices are consistent with decentralised decision-making necessary for profit-centre management. However, despite the assertion of Company 3 that market conditions result in a competitive transfer, negotiated transfer prices do not appear to be acceptable to the Inland Revenue (unless a comparable published price between unrelated parties can be identified). Company 3 is concerned that the Inland Revenue is in a position in which it can claim the 'benefit of hindsight', even though companies might have acted in a reasonable manner at the time of a decision.

6.5 Conclusions

Chapters 5 and 6 need to be considered in conjunction to illustrate how MNEs implement their transfer-pricing policies (with particular reference to the TPM adopted) and how they might gain assurance that these transfer-pricing policies will be acceptable to the fiscal authorities. Chapter 6 provides some general illustrations of the broad methods adopted for different intra-group transactions (e.g. profit split for financial services; cost-plus or resale-minus for products; and the allocation of central services at cost or cost plus a mark-up for value-added activities) and an example of one approach not recognised by the Inland Revenue (i.e. negotiation). Furthermore, each of the three MNEs discussing products had to place these transactions within the context of the corporate structure and other relevant intra-group transactions in their entirety. Chapter 5 demonstrated that MNEs might have formal relationships (e.g. APAs) or informal understandings with fiscal authorities which might increase their levels of assurance about the acceptability of their international transfer pricing.

The main message of Chapters 5 and 6 is that increased globalisation and the increasing influence of MNEs will ensure that the importance and profile of international transfer pricing will continue to grow. MNEs must continue to provide ever-improving supporting documentation to be able to respond to more stringent transfer-pricing regulations (in many countries) and more co-operation between different fiscal authorities.

On the one hand, it has been suggested that the high compliance costs will fall on non-US groups, groups with no experience in the USA and medium-sized firms looking at ITP for the first time (Company 4). However, sophisticated and experienced MNEs will face high compliance costs, particularly when a comparable price cannot be identified. In these cases, it is envisaged that in the future it will become more necessary to carry out or commission economic studies and database studies to justify prices, rather than rely on one specific method (Company 7).

One of the startling aspects which emerged from the interviews with participants who had experienced UK or US fiscal reviews or audits was the length of time the process can take. Transactions which occurred three or four years previously (or longer) remain subject to discussion between the companies and fiscal authorities. For these companies, whether because of established formal or informal links or faith in their documentation, an almost relaxed attitude appeared to exist to the investigation. This is unlikely to apply to those MNEs that have yet to have their documentation and ITP process tested by fiscal review.

7

Trends and Issues

At most, this fieldwork study represents one small step to obtain an enhanced appreciation of the issues surrounding ITP in the new era of corporate tax self-assessment. The scale of importance that our participating MNEs associate with ITP is evidenced by the links they made to corporate strategy, internal structures, relationships with fiscal authorities and the efforts expended to justify current pricing methods. ITP may therefore be interpreted as a core consideration in effectively operating their business globally. We are grateful to them for their participation, their openness and their patience in discussing what must have seemed relatively naive questions at times.

Some caution must be expressed when evaluating the implications of this research. First, the conscious decision to focus on a single, cross-border transaction of the participating MNE's choice means that the description offered may not be typical of other intra-group transactions in a single enterprise. The benefit of this approach, however, is that a level of detail and richness is obtained which in the best examples places ITP in a relevant organisational context. Second, the research is exploratory and therefore subject to our interpretation and potential bias. This was controlled by returning our report of the interview to the appropriate participant for authentication and accuracy checks. Finally, while the feedback process enabled participants to respond to follow-on questions, triangulation of data sources did not prove feasible within the timescale of the research. Also, the study considered ITP in each company at one point in time and could not incorporate any changes over time.

With these limitations in mind, the following trends and issues are identified.

7.1 Commercial versus fiscal reality

When a participating MNE chose to describe a cross-border transaction which related to a core business activity, we quickly recognised that not one but several transactions must be included in our examination. The co-ordination of subsidiaries in different geographic locations is essential whether the transaction is in the financial services, product or service sectors. Sequential interconnectedness or joint responsibility requires a recognition of environments with different regulations, corporate strategy and an awareness that the substance rather than form of transactions is the appropriate focus to take. In other words, several of the MNEs operate with global commerciality as a prime aim, although some of the participants did stress the importance of tax-efficient structures. This may be in contrast with the perspective that fiscal authorities must, of necessity, take.

Home and host tax inspectors are primarily concerned with their particular national jurisdiction. They are responsible for obtaining a fair share of taxation revenue for a national government. However, there is some evidence of information sharing by fiscal authorities to understand better the operations of and the disclosures by MNEs in the global market.

To alleviate this potential conflict, a reappraisal of the competent authority arrangements under the OECD Double Taxation Convention model may be appropriate and was mentioned by several participants. In similar vein, the EU Arbitration Convention may usefully allow fiscal authorities to increase the flow of shared information in order that global markets are fully understood and appreciated.

Several of the participating MNEs demonstrated that a close relationship with fiscal authorities has been and is being maintained. In specific instances, MNEs consult with tax inspectors to gain informal advice or regularly provide listings of intra-group transactions for the fiscal authorities. This dialogue, which appears to be well established in some companies and industry sectors, must over time educate all parties as to the commercial and fiscal realities of undertaking global trade. Similarly, there is a close relationship between their specialist big-five advisers and the Inland Revenue, for example. Many transfer-pricing advisers are ex-Inland Revenue and thus understand how fiscal authorities operate.

7.2 Organisation of fiscal authorities

The burden placed on fiscal authorities is immense and is reflected by the lapse of time between the actual transaction taking place and a tax settlement being reached. Anecdotal evidence of 1992 transactions being investigated in 1999 may be extreme but certainly the time lapse runs into years, with even sophisticated fiscal authorities, such as the IRS and IR, having considerable backlogs of work. The pressures are increasing with many fiscal authorities now offering MNEs the opportunity to enter into APAs.

The findings of this study suggest that different forms of transaction may have a relationship with the different ITP methods employed. In the financial services sector, profit split appears to be the method frequently used. For intra-group product transactions, transaction-based methods, such as cost plus a mark-up or resale price methods are preferred. Actual or standard cost plus a mark-up (the mark-up depends on the nature of the service provided) appears to be favoured by MNEs in the services-provision sector. These differences are substantiated, to a degree, by the different complexity, internal structures and managerial reward schemes the MNEs in the different sectors display.

If these patterns are typical, then reorganisation of fiscal authorities' internal structures may be a necessary and beneficial result. Tax inspectors who specialise in the financial services sector, for example, may not only build upon their sector experience but also bring to any discussions authoritative knowledge of the profit-split method. There is some indication of this trend in the UK Inland Revenue, where the long-established Oil Taxation Office within the International Division is generally well regarded by the appropriate participants in this study. The recently created Large Business Unit may be an illustration of this trend continuing.

7.3 Compliance costs

The burden placed on MNEs is immense. Uncertainty is also high, with tax reviews remaining open for many years; furthermore, it is not clear when closed years are truly closed. Many of the participating MNEs in the fieldwork have experience of dealing with fiscal authorities over a number of years. In some instances, this extends to reviews and even audits. It is also apparent that their internal tax departments are not newly created, but they are expanding. Despite uncertainty and compliance costs, there is a broad range of opinion on the merits of APAs.

This does not appear to be related to the form of individual transaction, industry sector or nationality of the parent company. The recently published recommendations on APAs in the UK may help MNEs to evaluate the relative benefit of adopting this approach. Undoubtedly, a clear specification of when and under which circumstances the fiscal authorities believe an APA would be useful to a MNE may improve the take-up rate. Also, any description of a generic APA or of the type of disclosure fundamental to succeed in obtaining an APA would be regarded as useful. However, the study has illustrated the uniqueness of corporate structure and flows, particularly for products. The potential for less formal and less rigorously assessed agreements, perhaps advance pricing understandings, may pave the way to closer co-operation between taxpayer and tax collector in future, although their reliability would depend on the level of understanding between MNE and fiscal authority, because unless the fiscal authority comprehends the MNE's flows, it cannot provide assurance.

One of the potential obstacles to increased adoption of APAs appears to be the likelihood of higher compliance costs. Functional analysis by an external economist expert in the field and the employment of specialist law firms to manage the process are incremental costs over and above the normal documentation and substantiation required under self-assessment. This study suggests that, owing to the inherent complexity in certain sectors, such as manufacturing, these normal costs are non-trivial. The apparent simultaneous occurrence of ITP relating to product flows and royalties in these cases suggests that compliance costs do not fall evenly on all taxpayers.

7.4 Conclusions

In many respects this research is path clearing. Along several lines, the issues surrounding ITP are distinguished from domestic transfer pricing. In fact, at no point did any of the twelve participants refer to domestic TP. Managerial rewards are decoupled from the financial performance measures of subsidiaries which may be contaminated by ITP following a different purpose. Regulated environments require MNEs to adopt different structures in different parts of the world. Fiscal authorities represent part of the regulated environment and legitimately require access to relevant ITP documentation. Thus, the issues we have highlighted, i.e. the global versus fiscal perspective, the MNE–fiscal authority relationship and compliance costs, are specific to ITP. Each indicates fertile areas for future research.

Certainly within the UK, very large MNEs, big-five advisers and the Inland Revenue are desperately trying to expand the number of ITP specialists employed. All

MNEs will need to consider their ITP policies, and perhaps the best defence is to have better documentation and systems in place than other MNEs. It is possible that those MNEs with little or no documentation, or less convincing justifications, will be the first targets for IR investigation. Many of the MNEs in the study have had experience of ITP – either because they are US MNEs, have US subsidiaries or operate in highly regulated industries.

Appendix 1: Summaries of the Twelve Interviews

Company 1

This US group manufactures and distributes a specific product. It operates with a number of 'divisions', including a European headquarters 'division', and manufacturers in a number of European countries. The UK is the site of the oldest and probably the biggest factory in Europe. The ITP policy is centrally determined by the US group. It is a simple, standard, fixed rate that applies to all final products (cost plus 5 per cent) and it has been stable at this rate for many years (effectively it is 'set in stone'). The rationale used to support the policy is that if the global return on the product is 10 per cent, then it is reasonable to share that between the manufacturer and the distributor. To date this has not been tested in the USA by the IRS.

The specific transaction: life cycle of the product

It is difficult to limit the analysis to one specific transaction for what is essentially a vertically integrated process. Instead, this report follows the sequence of 'transactions' relating to the specific product. The series of internal transactions for the specific product start with R&D and finish with transfers to the final distributors. The full sequence of intra-group transactions consists of R&D, supply of raw materials, manufacture of an intermediate product, manufacture of a final product, and distribution of the final product.

Structure of group/distinct stages for product

- *R&D.* The US group performs the pure research (there is a royalty charge of 5 per cent on all third-party sales that is paid to the USA for R&D). This 5 per cent figure is supported by two sources: (1) the main competitor has disclosed publicly that it uses a 5 per cent rate; and (2) to defend an enquiry by the German tax authorities, an independent expert certified that this rate was reasonable.
- *R&D.* There is also one research centre in Europe which performs research specific to the European market (this is funded by the USA on a cost basis out of the 5 per cent royalties paid by all group affiliates).
- Central materials purchasing team. This negotiates bulk purchases of raw materials for all European manufacturers to benefit from economies of scale. Therefore, for some raw materials the European HQ company agrees the price with suppliers and manufacturers place their orders direct with these suppliers (same cost to all European manufacturers, but variable distribution costs). For other

raw materials the European HQ company supplies them to the European group at cost plus 5 per cent. All manufacturers inform the European HQ company of their production requirements and then the European HQ company consolidates all the orders and ensures that sufficient raw materials and intermediate products are available.

- *Intermediate products.* Some of the intermediate products are manufactured only in the European HQ company and then supplied to all the European manufacturers. These products are proprietary and cannot be sourced externally (transferred at cost plus 5 per cent).
- *Manufacturers.* These typically manufacture a range of products – different manufacturers will concentrate on different ranges. This means that there are high levels of cross-border transactions, with manufacturers of a specific product supplying the manufacturers/distributors based in other European countries. The UK manufacturer is a net exporter of final products to Europe (the final product is transferred at scheduled cost plus 5 per cent – in exceptional circumstances, for market penetration in a new market or a market dominated by a competitor, cost plus 3 per cent has been used).
- *Central services.* These are arranged in the European HQ company and include sales and marketing; setting prices; IT services; financial services.
- *European headquarters.* This sets the sales prices into the market for the finished product on a European basis. These prices represent the minimum sales price at which the product can be sold into the market by the distributors. These prices can only be breached with written permission. They are set after compiling a 'Euro-cost' which aggregates the manufacturing costs across all the European factories.
- *Margin structure.* There is a very different margin structure across the range of products and across different countries, but the argument is that they average out to the standard mark-up.

Fiscal authorities/documentation/compliance

There has been a protracted transfer pricing enquiry with the Inland Revenue (for years in the late 1980s to mid-1990s) which is soon to be finalised. The documentation and compliance costs associated with this enquiry have been extremely onerous – documenting all internal/external purchases/sales. The intention is to agree/negotiate a settlement with the Inland Revenue in the near future. The company policy has been to use transfer pricing specialists from the local office of the external advisers, not from the central London unit.

The Inland Revenue has asked questions about a number of issues. For instance:

- Inter-company services are charged on a cost-only basis with no mark-up. The Inland Revenue has questioned why there is no mark-up on services provided by the UK to the rest of the European group.
- Interest rates on intra-group loans have been queried.

- The main thrust of the Inland Revenue enquiry does not question the cost plus 5 per cent policy itself – instead, it requires some evidence that the stated policy is in fact applied; and asks when the policy is not applied (i.e. exceptions). It is suggested that less than 1 per cent of transfers need to be individually negotiated because the margins are very low or even loss-making.

Similar enquiries to those made by the Inland Revenue have also been lodged by the tax authorities in Germany and Japan.

Euro

At the moment, the UK company is investigating the likely effect of the euro on market prices and transfer prices. Certain large customers will require their suppliers to invoice in euros, so the European group will need to have euro pricing across Europe.

Cost

Initial investigations have identified that the cost of producing similar products in different countries can vary substantially. These differences might affect which products are manufactured in which countries. Cost is based on traditional overhead apportionment with full schedule cost (including raw materials; labour; 'everything').

Transfer of raw materials/intermediate manufacture

- Commodity – this is grown and sourced by a specialist group company and transferred into the group at cost plus 5 per cent. The majority is bought in at spot prices. The cost is a weighted cost of home-grown and purchased prices.
- Standard intermediate product – manufactured and supplied by the European HQ company at cost plus 5 per cent.
- Specialist intermediate product – bought in by the group because it is too expensive to change the set-up or not economic to make). The European HQ company negotiates with suppliers on behalf of the group and then produces a monthly list of recommended suppliers and prices (it does not charge a mark-up for this).
- Other raw materials – negotiated by the European HQ company with external suppliers but then ordered by each subsidiary direct from the supplier. The purchases are agreed by regional services and then the salaries of these five people are recharged out to the manufacturers (at cost) on the basis of tonnage purchased.

Subsidiary management motivation/reward

There are two measures:

- reaching budgeted profit;
- cash flow – the excess cash which can be remunerated to the US parent. This is because (a) the group emphasises shareholder value analysis; and (b) the importance of cash was highlighted by a takeover defence.

Company 2

The parent company is based in the UK with 80 subsidiaries or more located worldwide and significant operating companies in the UK, USA, Brazil and Germany. The operating companies are distinguished because each holds trademarks or brands which are subject to royalty payments, and each company carries out the relevant product development R&D. Each brand covers a variety of products which are also sold and distributed globally. All the trademarks and brands employ the same technology for manufacture, and R&D, technical and advisory services are the subjects of transfer-pricing agreements. Concentration on a specific transaction of product flow therefore automatically involves consideration of additional intangible flows.

Strategic considerations

The group has adopted a product–market strategy which selectively matches brands with geographic regions or countries. This is in contrast with the previous strategy where subsidiaries may have competed in the same geographic market. The change has required greater co-ordination from the centre, not only in targeting brands to particular markets but also in the provision of technical, R&D, legal and taxation services. The current method of operations, which has applied for three years, is the focus of our attention. We concentrate on the significant operating companies, which each hold international brands (referred to in this summary as 'brand-holders'), although it should not be forgotten that other, smaller subsidiaries also manufacture products which compete with the international brands but only in a local market.

The transfer-pricing situations

The brand-holders' output flows to the UK group which then markets and sells on to subsidiaries in other parts of the world or to independent distributors. The UK group is the largest intermediary but does not deal with 100 per cent of the markets. The UK group contracts for the production at a transfer price of standard cost plus 10 per cent. A royalty of 5 per cent is paid to the brand-holder on all sales made by the UK group. The UK group is responsible for marketing and setting prices of international brands in specific regions or countries. Negotiation with subsidiaries producing local brand output is necessary to position the international brand at an appropriate price. Thus, when international brands are sold to independent distributors overseas, the margin of profit flows back to the UK group from which royalty and transfer-pricing fees are paid to the brand-holders. When sold to subsidiaries, the standard cost plus 10 per cent and 5 per cent royalty are borne by the subsidiary which deals with that particular market and captures the residual income.

Some deviation in the normal transfer-pricing policy occurs: for example, when the purchasing subsidiary is at the start-up stage of development, the 10 per cent plus is reduced. When a factory in a country is closed, it may be politic to ship products at a transfer price which maintains that subsidiary's profit performance.

The previous policy allowed brand-holders to receive the full revenue but resulted in time-consuming negotiations with other subsidiaries and, more importantly, resulted in increased competition between group brands in some markets. The change to the present standard cost plus 10 per cent and royalty fee policy was developed, and is justified in terms of the US company position by economic analysis. This justification does not address the worldwide position but provides some comfort to the companies operating in other countries. The functional analysis included the cost savings to brand-holders of no longer maintaining sales offices or representatives around the world. Under the current system, point-of-sale marketing is the responsibility of the company actually responsible for any given market. Marketing and maintaining the global image of a brand remains the responsibility of the individual brand-holder which, in part, justifies the royalty payment.

The functional analysis is performed annually but not necessarily on all markets and, although not tested by any fiscal authority as yet, the economists believe that the policy can be upheld if audited by the IRS. Likewise, the IRS regulations on document retention are now policy for all subsidiaries in the group. The group tax department is instrumental in communicating the policy to all finance directors in the subsidiaries, and for obtaining information on intra-group transactions: 'This is the policy that we follow for US purposes and we feel that this will be good enough anywhere else.' As an added assurance, the economists have conducted a longitudinal study over past years, applying a residual profit-split method. This justifies the cost-plus policy, so the IRS can be satisfied on the profit-split method while the OECD should accept the cost-plus method. An APA is not contemplated at this time, but the need for multilateral fiscal regulations to be taken into account is obvious.

Intangibles, other than those relating to brands, are also subject to transfer pricing. For example, the UK group provides technical and advisory services for all subsidiaries. These are charged out worldwide on a time basis. Every member of staff at group headquarters annually submits a breakdown of time spent working for subsidiaries. Increases in group costs from unforeseen expansion, or litigation and accompanying legal costs, form part of the technical and advisory services charged.

No profit is charged out (i.e. services are at cost) and the UK Inland Revenue audit this procedure once every three years, examining a block of three years at a time. This policy is acceptable to the IR, but internal conflicts arise when group personnel have been working on a subsidiary but not at the request of that subsidiary manager. Apparently attributable, but not charged, costs tend to rise (which are at present being looked at by the UK company) and exchange controls may make payment by the subsidiary difficult, if not impossible. Adjustment of the transfer-pricing policy may be considered in these cases. The only difference between the two instances is that there is a transfer-pricing adjustment in the UK tax computations for the first instance.

With the change in strategy, group strategic/consumer affairs R&D is now exclusively undertaken in the UK. Product development R&D is undertaken by the brand-owners (including Germany, the USA and Brazil) which then make charges to the markets which have benefited. Again, costs are charged out to subsidiaries and the process is designed to qualify as a cost-sharing arrangement under US regulations. This gives the assurance that, once reviewed by the IRS and accepted, the general principles of s482 to investigate earlier years no longer applies. The basis of sharing group strategic R&D costs is on subsidiary turnover, and this also complies with OECD guidelines. Product development R&D costs are charged on a fee basis.

A further transfer-pricing situation relates to the basic raw material each manufacturing subsidiary requires. Purchasing is arranged centrally by the UK group (but the UK team responsible does not take title) which charges a 3 per cent commission for the service to the subsidiaries. At first glance, the application of a comparable uncontrolled price may appear appropriate, but the raw material has several grades and the brand-holders and product may require up to 25 different types of raw material.

Internal arrangements

The company has hundreds of agreements which relate to these flows of tangibles and intangibles. For all appropriate parties, there are technical and advisory, R&D, central purchasing, royalty agreements relating to trademarks and brands and, of course, end-product transfer agreements. Within the group, these involve tax specialists, trademark lawyers, senior finance personnel from the brand holders and other high-ranking personnel when policy is changed. Subsidiary managers are also obviously involved in specific agreements. When dealing with the tax authorities of jurisdictions overseas, local advisers (generally accounting practitioners) act on behalf of the local subsidiary. This has not changed with the change in strategy.

Taxation considerations

The variation in the standard cost plus transfer price may be contemplated when customs and excise policy in a particular country is considered. This may also be catered for by changing the structure and interfacing a separate marketing company in a specific flow, say.

With an overall objective of global profit maximisation, repatriation of cash and dividends is another consideration. While a monthly cash netting-off system operates for all intra-group transactions, differential tax rates and foreign tax credit regimes have an influence. A combination of the abolition of advance corporation tax (ACT) in the UK and the controlled foreign company legislation has led to other forms of netting-off being explored. For example, a subsidiary under a zero income tax or tax holiday regime pays UK tax in full because there is no foreign tax credit. A subsidiary with a 50 per cent income tax liability overseas does not pay UK tax, but much of the foreign tax credit is wasted. However, if these dividends from different subsidiaries come into one offshore company, the national income tax rates are blended and if that approximates the UK rate, maximum use of tax credits is made. In order to realise these benefits, a comprehensive examination of the tax laws in the offshore company jurisdiction and its relationship with other countries where subsidiaries are located is required, as well as the IR rates. Capital gains tax, withholding tax, capital duty and income tax differentials need to be considered. While the 'blender' arrangement took several months to create internally, the three fiscal authorities gave opinions supporting the arrangement within weeks.

The ACT influence can be considerable, creating effective income tax differentials such as 11 per cent, 38 per cent or 45 per cent: 'You can't ignore big differentials like that and where you've got locations where you've got tax holidays or special tax deals, we do take advantage of them.'

Performance measurement and managerial compensation

Subsidiaries and subsidiary management are evaluated on several performance dimensions, including effective marketing, sales volume, and repatriated cash to the UK. Technical and advisory services, royalty, etc., arrangements contribute to the cash-back measure. Occasionally, the tax department acts as arbiter when a treatment which is tax advantageous for the group has an adverse effect on the subsidiary's performance. This is alleviated in two ways. First, a distinction can be made between performance indicators, reflecting the manager's as opposed to the subsidiary's effectiveness. Secondly, when the group benefit reduces a manager's performance measure, a profit-relief system operates to demonstrate the reason for apparent underachievements.

Subsidiary managers' targets are expressed in pounds sterling and, even though their internal reports are in local currency, currency exposure is the responsibility of the managers. In addition, the transfer price is based on standard costs, with conventional absorption of overheads. The intention is to ensure that cost inefficiencies are not passed on via the transfer-pricing policy.

Wish list

In terms of providing documentary and economic evidence to justify the transfer-pricing policies, the participant believed the group to be 'set up to our best possible advantage'. However, the entire system had yet to be tested by fiscal audit and inevitably some jurisdictions may win but others lose.

Themes

A significant presence in the USA has increased awareness of the US transfer-pricing regulations which appear to have provided guidance, if not the benchmark, for documentation within the total group. More recently, the group is also taking note of the UK developments.

The change in strategy affected the transfer-pricing policy and the way the subsidiaries interrelated. While the investment in physical assets is highly specific, production utilisation/effectiveness in the end-product market, not economies of scale, provided the reason for change. Effectiveness in end-product markets and to eliminate unnecessary and wasteful inter-subsidiary competition are the chosen missions. Of necessity, a greater degree of co-ordination from the centre and a reappraisal of different subsidiaries' risks resulted in a different transfer-pricing policy as well as more service and intangible provision subject to transfer prices. However, following the successful changes in terms of end markets, the group is now implementing changes to address economies of scale.

The complexities of dealing in many tax jurisdictions with different forms of taxation and differential rates, place transfer pricing in context. Transfer pricing-policy is potentially influenced by these other tax considerations, notwithstanding that documentary and economic justification can be given.

Company 3

The specific transaction

The specific transaction relates to the provision of freight services. The company has a UK subsidiary which (among other functions) can provide transportation services within and outside the group. Likewise, other affiliates can source their requirements within or outside the group. In 1993, a French affiliate informed the commercial department in the UK that it required three vessels of 21,000 tonnes and the commercial department duly tendered for the business.

One independent party provided a quote of $160,000 per voyage. The UK bid matched the quote and was duly awarded the contract by the French affiliate. When the Oil Taxation Office (OTO), a section of the Inland Revenue (IR), questioned the transfer price, the independent quote was offered as a comparable uncontrolled price on the basis that it represented 'convincing and compelling evidence'. The fiscal authority then argued that a transfer price of £7.60 per tonne should replace the actual transfer price of £6.90 per tonne. The IR freight rate calculation was based on the 21,000 tonne capacity, whereas the commercial department had assumed that the independent third-party bid used vessels capable of carrying 23,000 tonnes. The IR argued that the tender document stated 21,000 tonnes although, in practice, independent parties often vary the terms of the vessel's capacity, the important issue being the capability to execute the contract with whatever size of cargo is required.

The UK taxpayer has argued that if the transfer price had not matched the comparable uncontrolled price, then the French affiliate could legitimately have accepted the independent party's bid. All related parties are profit centres and intra-group trades of this kind are generally subject to intensive negotiation between them.

At this time the dispute with the IR remains unresolved.

Freight rates 1993–5

The transfer-pricing methods used to compute freight rates have varied due to market conditions. Generally, contracts are in force for one year.

The 1993 method relied on the independent quote. In 1994, no independent quote was available; instead, a market forecast of freight rates from Clarksons, a shipping broker, and the London Trader Broker Panel was used. At the year end, this forecast proved to be equivalent to the actual market rate and, following correspondence, was agreed with the IR.

In 1995, a similar method to that used in 1993 was again employed. This is subject to ongoing correspondence with the IR.

Market conditions obviously influence the negotiation process. In 1993, demand for vessels was low, and if the intra-group trade had not taken place, the ships would have been left idle, in all likelihood, or sold. The vessels in question carry 'dirty' cargoes which limit their versatility. To be switched to other transportation uses would involve significant cleaning costs. Hence, the nature of the market makes one-year regular contract work highly desirable. Market conditions therefore suggest that a competitive transfer price is required.

Contact with the IR

There is a well-established relationship between the OTO, which maintains a database on all oil companies, and the UK affiliate's own tax department. This is normal for the industry overall. Each year, transfer-pricing enquiries are received from the OTO, and it is now normal practice for the details of all intra-group transactions to be provided to the OTO (not limited to freight).

Differing perspectives appear to exist. For example, the taxpayer argues that each cargo has different proportions of product of different quality, dependent on the source; hence a universal freight rate is not applicable. However, a long-term rate for the same cargo may be appropriate, dependent on market conditions. The OTO does not accept negotiation as an appropriate transfer-pricing method. Because of the profit-centre management philosophy, the company decentralises some transfer pricing to the affiliates via a process of detailed negotiation. Each affiliate takes decisions on its own business – subject to a general-interest override. In this specific case, the decision-making power had been passed to the affiliate concerned and no general interest overrides took place.

General

With the introduction of the proposed new UK legislation and corporate tax self-assessment, there are considerable concerns about related compliance costs. Intra-group transactions are numerous, and it is unclear whether any underlying agreements exist or particular transfer-pricing methods are favoured. The tax department first needs to understand the nature of all intra-group transactions. Compliance with the detail contained in the consultative document/proposed new legislation may result in the grouping of transactions into product or service families to justify different transfer-pricing policies. Functional analysis may be utilised in this process, although no extensive use is made at present. It is not contemplated that APAs will be sought. APAs are viewed as 'time-consuming and it is arguing before the event'.

A further difference of opinion relates to the European Arbitration Convention. It appears that the IR interprets a transfer-price adjustment as needed before the convention can be invoked. Some other European tax jurisdictions believe that it is triggered by a transfer-price enquiry itself. More importantly, the Inland Revenue appears to have a very restricted view on the circumstances in which the convention can apply.

Tensions

The primary tension relates to the company's management philosophy of profit-centre management. This is justified by the dynamic market conditions which affiliates in the group face and the need to maintain decentralised decision-making. Negotiated transfer prices are consistent with this approach but do not appear to be acceptable to the fiscal authority (unless they can identify a comparable published price between unrelated parties): 'A more realistic and commercial approach by the IR' is a primary requirement. The IR, on the other hand, requires detailed documentation after the event to justify the transfer prices used. One of the concerns is that the IR is in a position in which it can claim the 'benefit of hindsight', even though companies might have acted in a reasonable manner at the time of a decision.

Company 4

The specific transaction

The specific transaction relates to the manufacture and distribution of a new product. The company operates in a highly regulated global industry which appears to have influenced the organisational structure, the flow of internal transactions and, consequently, the implications for transfer pricing. R&D is of great significance, and when a compound (product) is discovered it is immediately patented. Of the seventeen years of the patent, perhaps six years will elapse before the product comes to market.

Structure of group/distinct stages for the new product

- A UK group company owns all intellectual property and under a contract agreement pays one of its subsidiaries, a research company, for all R&D on a cost-plus basis (expenses plus 10 per cent). The UK company which pays for the intellectual property commercially exploits it. The *intellectual property* company grants a licence to all other companies and receives a royalty based on a fair return (e.g. it grants a manufacturing licence to the primary manufacturers and the secondary manufacturers); clearing company – granted rights to sell to approved companies; distributors granted rights.

- *Primary manufacture* is carried out in one of two countries – the UK or the Far East. The UK group grants manufacturing authorisation to the primary manufacturing company through a formal licensing agreement. Therefore, as well as investing in specific assets, the primary manufacturers pay royalties to the UK to fund all future R&D. Once set, the royalties appear not to change and are kept uniform. The primary manufacturer then sells to a European clearing company. This is essentially a reinvoicing operation. The European clearing company bears the currency risk and charges a small mark-up agreed by the tax authorities in that country – working back from the resale price and providing the European company with an agreed percentage of its turnover (the European clearing company buys products at a fixed price from both primary manufacturers which is set by the UK HQ).

- The *secondary manufacturers* (e.g. the centre of excellence for aerosol manufacturer) are licensed to manufacture and then they sell everything back to the clearing house which then sells to the marketing subsidiaries.

- The *European clearing company* sells the finished products to subsidiaries in all the different markets at individual/different prices based on the market conditions of each market. The vast majority of the companies are marketing companies alone (i.e. primary/secondary manufacture is done elsewhere and these companies buy the finished products from the European clearing company – the transfer price charged by the European clearing company to the distributors is based on resale-minus). Local subsidiary management can contact a special

'Commercial Unit' if special circumstances exist (e.g. local trading conditions; change in product life cycle) to negotiate a different transfer price. In turn, the Commercial Unit can agree this with the European clearing company. The Commercial Unit is involved with setting all transfer prices – the Commercial Unit is involved when the intellectual property department grants rights, and sets the initial transfer prices according to risks/rewards and trade conditions. In effect, the Commercial Unit is an arm of the clearing company and acts as a facilitator between the subsidiaries and the clearing company. It usually reviews transfer prices quarterly.

- Resale-minus has been selected for a number of reasons:
  - ◇ nearly every market in the world is regulated – this means that the host regulatory bodies often fix the final selling price; in the UK, an industry regulatory body determines that the profit-split method is not a possibility;
  - ◇ there are different prices appropriate to each market;
  - ◇ the cost of manufacture is a very small proportion of the value of the final product – this is why cost-plus is not used.

The UK sets the negotiated price retrogressively and the others set prices in advance.

The ITP policy is centrally determined and administered – this is essential because of the highly regulated environment of the industry. This necessity is reflected by the long-established internal tax department at HQ. In addition to regulatory requirements, the ITP policy needs to take into account product life cycle and local market conditions, allowing limited potential for negotiation. All enquiries from fiscal authorities anywhere in the world are dealt with by the UK group. This ensures that there is consistency throughout the world and that a uniform calculation is used. This approach is necessary because of increased global transparency: 'Authorities talk to each other.'

Performance evaluation of the marketing subsidiaries

Local managers are evaluated on the profit generated in their company. As such, they will seek to both set the best in-market price and spend sterling on promotion/selling expenses most efficiently. For subsidiaries which distribute and do not manufacture, advertising and promotion are important items in their budget. The gross margin to subsidiaries is in a range which is open to bargaining (through the Commercial Unit), and which takes into account the functions and risks of the subsidiary. Managers are rewarded on meeting budgeted targets and maximising sales – but there is the facility to negotiate with the 'commercial team' if something unusual happens.

Functional analyses

For the past five or six years, annual functional analyses have been carried out to update initial analyses in the USA. In the UK, there has been a small functional analysis for newer products (since 1992–3). In addition, there have been similar analyses in Australia and (possibly) Canada.

Functional analysis is an essential building block in securing an APA. Having a bilateral or multilateral agreement for a five-year period offers certainty, but some authorities focus on each individual transaction while the group would prefer a grouping (or basket) of transactions approach (as supported by the OECD).

Documentation/compliance

Documentation and compliance costs are increasing, especially in relation to functional analysis. It is estimated that 50 per cent of the tax department's time (seven professionals) is devoted to ITP issues. However, once initial compliance costs have been met it should not be too expensive to maintain these documentation requirements. Furthermore, the group is confident that documentation is available to uphold current ITP methods.

The group sends annually to the IRS a 'statement of fact' listing all inter-affiliate transactions. There is a likelihood that, as fiscal authorities increase their networking, similar 'statements' might need to be provided to show to the fiscal authorities. This may be to the benefit of all parties, especially if the competent authority procedures can be improved or 'polished'.

External advisers are used for *ad hoc* assignments, but the costs involved suggest that further strengthening of the internal provision might be more effective.

It is suggested that the high compliance costs will fall on non-US groups, groups with no experience in the USA and medium-sized firms looking at ITP for the first time.

If there is one aspect of ITP which would improve your level of assurance of meeting tax authority enquiries, what would it be?

'Certainty is key' – anything that increases the level of certainty/reduces the danger of different tax authorities all attacking a company. Also, the 'competent authority' procedure is a protracted process that needs improving (especially as there is likely to be a '10/20-fold increase in cross-border transactions').

Euro

Little impact is expected on ITP policy as a result of the introduction of the euro. If anything, it will reduce price differentials and allow greater transparency.

Company 5

The specific transaction

The participating company focused on the agency-broking activity and, in particular, the purchase and sale of equities worldwide on behalf of institutional investors. The UK office is a subsidiary of a US parent with similar offices across the globe, including Japan and Hong Kong.

Approximately 40 per cent of the agency-broking activity is undertaken for UK clients using the London Stock Exchange and therefore does not involve transfer pricing. Intra-group transactions occur when, for example, a UK client wishes to purchase US equity or a Hong Kong client wishes to purchase UK equity. Inevitably, in any time period there is an imbalance in that the UK office may generate five times more clients for purchasers of US equities than the US office generates for the purchase of UK equities. There is need to recognise and reward those parts of the group which generate clients and those which execute purchases or sales on behalf of overseas clients. The group's aim is to provide a globally integrated equity-broking service to maximise overall profitability.

When a deal is completed, the executing office charges the generating office a transfer price for the work done. Prior to 1995, the transfer price was determined on a full cost-plus basis. The direct costs associated with the individual deal would have added to them a proportion of the executor office overhead. The overhead would be allocated on the basis of the percentage of business done that month for the sister subsidiary office. The mark-up would vary according to the marketplace: for example, commission rates in the Far East are higher than in the UK. This differential is explained by market development and the risk associated with various market prices. For purchasing transactions in, say, Hong Kong (i.e. similar deals), the mark-up is virtually the same except for 'underlying influences of the day'. Although still used as a secondary justification of the current transfer-pricing policy, the primary means of computation now relies on the comparable profit method (CPM).

From 1995, external advisers have helped the group to set transfer prices by the CPM. This is interpreted as, 'So if we had a company in this particular part of the world that was using a third party to transact business, what relative profit margins they were making on that style of business, given the data that was available.' The external advisers to the US office identified fifteen comparable businesses which, when size, turnover and geographical spread are addressed, whittled down to nine. The advisers carefully inspected these for loss-leading departments in order to derive relative profit margins. Hence, a generator office may expect a 9 or 10 per cent margin on business executed by other subsidiaries, subject to their location. CPM is now the group's policy on transfer-price determination, and the initial motivation came from the USA where the IRS has accepted it. Nevertheless, the documentary evidence of the full cost-plus process is maintained in order that fiscal challenges can be met.

APAs

The group's attitude is to react rather than proact in its involvement with fiscal agencies. While the similarities and frequencies of executing deals suggests that an APA may be appropriate, the relatively recent introduction of the CPM, together with the educational costs of becoming a globally integrated company, do not merit additional changes. With the changes in fiscal legislation worldwide, however, the possibility of beginning APA negotiations is not totally discounted. If this approach was adopted, a UK–global APA is the preferred form.

Managerial incentives

The educational process, of which transfer pricing is a part, de-emphasises the profitability measures as reflections of effectiveness. 'Investment tends to be at variable costs' in that the human assets are more significant than the value of buildings or properties. The most significant financial figure is the gross commissions flows, which suggest that generating deals is a key variable. However, commissions on inter-affiliate are lower than home-generated business, and there is no real discretion to use non-group subsidiaries to execute trades. Responsibility for subsidiary profit is therefore difficult to pinpoint.

Relationship with the IR

The external advisers who developed and maintain the CPM liaise with the IR, and this practice of using local independent advisers in different parts of the globe is the norm in the group. While it is a truly global operation, the group is not large in size of employees but it is a complex environment. The underlying nature of the business requires explanations to be given by local independent advisers. Obviously, income and corporate tax differentials are important considerations, although withholding tax and *ad valorem* taxes generally do not apply.

Euro

Some benefit is expected with the introduction of the euro, if only to reduce bank charges because there will be fewer currencies to be converted each month end. American clients will no longer be exposed to as many currencies fluctuating and, more importantly, country-based risks may be reduced by the European Union having a common currency. This will, in turn, reduce the number of comparables to be used in transfer-price determination.

Themes

The most significant step forward would be the establishment of 'an internationally accepted standard to give a level of assurance about a certain allocation being the norm'. This would also reduce the cost of employing advisers.

Fiscal considerations govern the transfer-pricing process, as reflected by the dual justification of CPM and full cost-plus methods.

Operating as a global business renders profit responsibility at local offices or subsidiaries unattainable because any intra-group deal involves a generator and an executor. The value added by either party is difficult to ascertain, but both parties are essential if deals are to be made.

Company 6

The specific transaction

There are two distinct businesses: (institutional) investment management and corporate finance. In both cases, the transfer-pricing issue concerns fee-splitting. How should the fee be divided between that part of the business that gets the client and that part of the business that does the work?

- *Investment management.* This is when a client invests some money in the firm and the firm manages this investment. In fact, there are about 40 countries which sell investment management services in the group but only six which have fund managers and research (including the UK, the USA and Hong Kong). The client-owner receives 75 per cent of the fee. This is an ongoing relationship with the client. The fund manager receives 25 per cent of the fee.
- *Corporate finance,* e.g. mergers and acquisitions; capital rating. The business introducing the client receives 25 per cent of the fee. The business doing the work receives 75 per cent of the fee. In some instances, where the client-owner also carries out some of the execution of the work, there is a case for a 50/50 split. The fees are normally split in blocks of 25 per cent. These splits are generally agreed as fair by the internal parties to the transactions.

One of the problems when considering any sort of profit split is that, although the USA and the UK make profits, some countries such as Asia make losses because, in general, clients are not prepared to pay much. Also, in particular global regions each particular business might be run as a single unit involving transactions in more than one country. In these cases, it is problematic allocating fees and expenses between companies in different countries.

If a business unit (e.g. a start-up in a new country) is expected to make a loss in early years, then these businesses (both European and Asian) are run at cost-plus to begin with (e.g. Scandanavia; Singapore) to avoid building up losses in smaller countries. This means that, in the initial stages, their costs determine their income. With a number of European countries, if during the year the business generates sufficient income, then they move from cost-plus to fee-splitting.

There is probably no such thing as a CUP in this industry – the fees bear no relation to the actual work done. However, it is possible to argue that this approach to fee-splitting is used by most other firms in the industry.

Central services (other than shareholders' costs) will be charged out on a headcount basis (which has to be kept for statutory accounts) in the future. Some of the low-margin affiliated businesses (e.g. photocopier leasing business) argue that this approach is inequitable.

Management accounts/bonuses

The business produces a set of worldwide management accounts to prevent arguments about remuneration/bonuses. Costs tend to follow income as the major component of cost is bonuses. In part, the management accounts are prepared on this basis to avoid arguments and wasting time and energy discussing how to split fees.

The emphasis of the business is moving towards operating as global functions. This means that the bonuses are related to the performance of the group function. This change has received opposition from the US firm, which has traditionally made very good profits (and therefore bonuses).

In the past, the corporate finance management accounts have shown the way in which fees have been split and the performance of individual businesses. But on the investment management side the management accounts have been reported on a global basis for years.

The purpose of the bonus is to reward good performance but, more importantly, to stop key players leaving the firm and joining a competitor. Therefore, even if a business is loss-making the bonus is still paid to stop them going elsewhere. Hence rewards/bonuses are not strictly related to subsidiary profit performance.

The UK is the base – it generates most business for both investment management and corporate finance in the UK. Likewise, for capital reasons, large-scale underwriting can only be done in the UK because the UK has the size and strength to be able to do that.

Longer-term strategies

Avoid making too much profit in countries with tax rates well over 30 per cent (e.g. the USA, Japan, Germany, Italy) and avoid making losses which cannot be relieved. Generally, many countries regulate the business such that investment management, securities and banking must be in separate companies. In some countries (e.g. Asia) the losses in one company cannot be offset against profits in another company.

Company 7

The specific transaction

The participating company is the headquarters of a UK group having subsidiaries in other parts of the world. The specific transaction relates to dealings in UK government stocks (particularly gilts). The majority of functions are located in London (capital; risk; research; settlement; execution) and most of the business originates in the UK with no transfer-pricing implications, but often sales originate overseas when clients of the European, Asian and North American offices want to trade in UK gilts. In these cases, 100 per cent of the income is generated in the UK (along with costs associated with execution), while the overseas offices will have a cost base (e.g. the sales team) but no income. The transfer-pricing decision is, what should the comparable, controlled price be that is paid to the overseas office for originating the business? For small-scale, established subsidiaries or start-up businesses within the group, the transfer price is cost-plus (usually cost plus 10 per cent).

The problem arises when the transfer prices need to be justified to the fiscal authorities. In these cases, if a comparable price cannot be identified, there is pressure to adopt a comparable profit-margin approach for the complete function. However, it is envisaged that in the future it will become more necessary to carry out or commission economic studies and database studies to justify prices, rather than rely on the cost-plus method.

The transfer-pricing system for well-established large subsidiaries is based on fee-splitting rather than direct product-cost allocation (e.g. systems and immediate support services, including product accounting and compliance), primarily for VAT reasons. Income generation is either exempt or zero rated, while moving costs might result in VATable importation services, for example. Considering other costs, the central management costs (e.g. central finance; HR; corporate communications) are allocated on a head-count or square-footage basis to the subsidiaries, while the shareholder costs should not be recharged at all. Note that for many transactions undertaken by financial institutions, they cannot be viewed in isolation but are linked with other types of transactions. For instance, a business might hedge a future against an exposed position on some stock, fixed income or equity.

APAs

The group is currently renegotiating an APA on swaps between the UK and the USA for the third time since the initial APA in 1991. In the past, any number from nine to eighteen IRS representatives have attended APA meetings. Often, these IRS representatives have not discussed the case beforehand to agree a common agenda. Each of the previous APAs has been for a three-year duration, and the APA is based on a subjective formula which takes into account front-office costs. The IRS is keen to ensure that companies cannot shift new transactions into the remit of the APA which had not been agreed to. Therefore, any movements between the domestic book and the APA book are time-stamped. The APA is a bilateral (rather than multilateral) agreement because it was hard enough to satisfy the two authorities: 'So the APA process is not one to be recommended. It is one to be recommended in terms of getting certainty if the numbers are big enough' or the area is complex enough. To date, the Germans have not been keen to negotiate an APA, so a cost plus 10 per cent policy is used in Germany. A possible bilateral agreement between the UK and Japan is being considered for the period beginning 1 January 1996 when the Japanese began to accept mark-to-market accounting.

Typically, although the swaps book is global and responsibility for the book moves around the world, traders are likely to concentrate on trading currencies and risk within their own time zones. Therefore, when the book moves to the USA it is unlikely that a great deal of decision-making will be carried out in respect of the European currencies in the book. The complete global book will be apportioned to all the centres which take some responsibility for it on a profit-split basis. This approach in relation to the centres is followed, even though some of the transactions might only involve specific centres (e.g. for UK/US transactions). Also, within the book, it is the back-office end (all the support systems, legal work, accounting) which is truly global and difficult to split up rather than the local costs of people.

Performance evaluation

The management accounts operate a system with different fee structures for different lines of business. In part, this is to incentivise traders to concentrate on those products which are harder to shift or those products which the group requires to be shifted. These incentives impact at the operating-desk level.

In addition, the management accounts are prepared on a global product basis (e.g. European government products around the world) which the manager can then break down into components (e.g. UK gilts). In terms of bonuses, the chief executive will share the total group bonus between the main companies and then these bonuses gradually filter down. It is very discretionary how they are divided between the different products and regions. For instance, managers will evaluate local market conditions and reward traders on the basis of whether or not there are opportunities to leave and join other firms ('If every trader in sight has been poached in Hong Kong and the thing's gone through the roof, then he'll take that into account'), in awarding a bonus.

In the case of the APA for the swaps book, the tax computation and the reward system are decoupled: 'essentially the APA is a calculation done for tax and that's it'. The APA is used to apportion profit for tax purposes, but traders are rewarded on an entirely different basis: for instance, what the group needs to pay traders in different countries to ensure that the traders do not join a competitor.

Tax losses

Another very important consideration is to ensure that tax losses are used before they expire. Sometimes a business transaction needs to be done to crystallise a profit in one year so that losses can be carried forward for a renewed period of time.

Relationship with the IR

The important thing to do under the new UK transfer-pricing legislation is to ensure good documentation that describes what the group is doing; what the issues are; how they are dealt with; and to be able to support the prices. If this documentation is in place, it is likely that the IR will concentrate on 'riskier' companies for the next five to ten years.

Nature of the business

One of the key aspects of the business is the efficient use of capital. The direction in which the IRS is heading is that functions should be rewarded on an arm's-length basis, and that any residual income after rewarding the various functions should be left where the risk lies.

> *If there is one aspect of ITP which would improve your level of assurance of meeting tax authority enquiries, what would it be?*
>
> I think the fiscal authority's approach in some cases is a bit over the top, but generally speaking they need to be satisfied in this sort of area as best they can. So you know, I've no great objections as long as the Revenue are being reasonable about these sorts of things to what we are being asked to do.
>
> And if I was going to name one thing in answer to your question which would be more relevant to this organisation than some others ... the whole of the business is run on pre-tax basis ... But where we are trying to sort out issues on transfer pricing, because it's hitting the tax line after the number they're judged on, it's very low down their priorities. And it's not just transfer pricing, there's lots of other things. We have to address it on some of our structured financial products which have a pre-tax loss and a first tax profit because they're not incentivised properly then. But yeah, if the business could move to a post-tax basis in looking at itself, transfer pricing would come much higher on their agenda and make our life easier in many respects.

Company 8

The specific transaction

In a comprehensive interview, the participating company's three main lines of business which involve international transfer pricing were discussed. All three are reported here in order to convey the variety and complexity of the global banking industry.

The participating company is the UK subsidiary of an American parent. The three operations identified are :

- provision of advice to a client by several subsidiaries in the group;
- trades in stocks, derivatives, etc., by one subsidiary which involve ancillary services being offered by a sister subsidiary;
- global book trading, where a number of subsidiaries provide and have joint and revolving responsibility for, say, trading of foreign exchange options, over any 24-hour period.

Advisory services

By way of illustration, we concentrate on advisory services provided by, say, an investment banking division which may be subdivided into corporate finance, which creates and maintains client relationships, and a mergers, acquisitions and restructuring department (the M&A department) which executes deals in accordance with clients' wishes.

For example, a Texan utilities company may want to take over a regional electricity company in the UK. Corporate finance personnel in New York may have cultivated a well-established relationship over several years before the Texan company reveals its intention. New York corporate finance will then contact the UK M&A team which has subgroups specialising in industry sectors. This UK-based utilities subgroup will then advise the Texan company of the best way of acquiring the utilities company, after conducting a due-diligence review. The plan of action for the acquisition may require finance, in which case the New York execution personnel will also become involved. Abstracting from the latter complication, the transfer-pricing issue concerns how much of the client fee should be recognised as coverage (client relationship) in New York and execution (research and advice) conducted in the UK.

Each case is idiosyncratic and comparable fees, either externally or internally, are unreliable because of the inevitable special circumstances affecting each of the advisory services. The group brought in an economist to try to determine the relative values of the services. In general, a 50/50 division is maintained, with half the revenue credited to New York (coverage) and half to the UK (execution). If, introducing the complication, New York also undertook some execution work, that part of the revenue is split further, leaving New York with 75 per cent and the UK with 25 per cent of the total fee.

The economist's solution employed functional analysis, and the transfer-pricing policy has operated since 1994. The explicit intention was to comply with the US regulations, especially s.482, but the policy is yet to be audited. This appears to be the case for many US companies in the sector which have introduced transfer-pricing policies in the last five years. Essentially, the detailed 60-page document containing the functional analysis will be used to uphold this company's policy and will be made available to fiscal authorities, including the International Division of the Inland Revenue.

The general policy has an exception when particular subsidiaries cannot offer a full advisory service, i.e. coverage and execution. In these circumstances, the transfer price is based on cost plus 10 per cent, with cost being the full cost, salaries and overheads of the smaller subsidiary or branch. The mark-up is consistently applied worldwide for all smaller subsidiaries, and the different tax jurisdictions have accepted this. When subsidiaries reach a certain size, the general policy then applies.

Trading with ancillary services

This involves trades undertaken in one location and ancillary services, reflecting a contribution offered by sister subsidiaries, in another location. For example, non-dollar swaps are risk-managed and traded in London by the UK subsidiary. Virtually all the operation's personnel are located in London, but all transactions are booked on to a US unregulated swaps entity in the group. The London-based traders and operations staff essentially enter into contracts on behalf of this US entity, so that all the revenue is shown against the US entity and the costs lie in the UK, at least initially.

As with any investment bank, the participating company is 'very very sensitive on capital and we try to use it as effectively as we can'. The unregulated US entity does not need to be capitalised itself because the parent company provides guarantees and cash-flow guarantees. The unregulated US swaps entity takes on the credit risk of the counterparty and the market risk. The group moves all the revenue from the US unregulated swaps entity to the UK. The profit then resides in the UK but then, in recognition of the market risk and credit risk (ancillary services) provided by the US swaps entity, a fee in the form of a transfer price is paid from London. Likewise, a transfer price in the form of a fee is paid by London to the parent company for the guarantee. In general terms, this may result in 95 per cent of the profits shown in the UK and 5 per cent in the USA.

To avoid potential problems with the IRS, the group is negotiating an APA which is described in detail later. The IRS appears to be 'trying to put an awful lot of value on capital, on the risk-taking in the US', and the protracted negotiations have lasted three years so far. The fees under the APA comprise 12.5 basis points on the notional amounts of the contract for the guarantee. This can be justified from separate external facilities with third-party banks. The credit- and market-risk fees are determined by using Monte Carlo simulations of the statistical likelihood of losing money on any particular swaps position. This allows the combination of various market- and credit-risk scenarios to determine expected losses. The fees (transfer prices) are based on those expected losses. Monte Carlo simulation is the market practice when pricing swaps with external parties, and the UK subsidiary's traders provided the input for applying the technique to the internal transactions.

Global book trading

For various transactions, such as option trading, the group has subsidiaries around the world which contain traders, operations and back-office support that are virtually identical. Instead of booking trades on to local entities, they all use a single unregulated US entity. When the markets close in one part of the globe, the book and the risk management for the positions move to a sister subsidiary where the markets are open. All profit is then located at the US entity and a transfer-pricing policy is needed to recognise the contribution which each individual subsidiary has made.

The IRS accepts a profit-split method as appropriate for this activity. Three factors are used to apply the profit split method:

- expertise of the traders, as measured by their relative compensation in each subsidiary;
- where the risk is borne, which is the USA where all transactions are booked;
- which subsidiaries provide operations or back-office functions to the trade, as measured by the relative salary costs in each subsidiary.

To determine the profit split, the traders' expertise has a weighting of 4, with the other factors having a weighting of 1 each. This displays the importance of the traders and allows a composite measure of each subsidiary's contribution to be measured.

The traders' relative compensation is fully weighted for their location, but such is their importance to the activity that 'management will make a judgement decision on how much they think particular traders are worth compared to one another'. When 'bonuses can amount to millions of dollars, cost of living doesn't enter into it, luckily for them'. This means that fiscal authorities can and do enquire about compensation and salary awards, but it is really only the group management which can assess the value of the individual, given track record, market pressures and other employment opportunities open to the traders. Perhaps the most potent defence of this basis of profit split is that any fiscal authority's estimate of appropriate compensation for a trader would be difficult to uphold.

Relationships with fiscal authorities

The financial sector in general, and the participant company as an example, has several different lines of business which are managed, if not globally, then regionally. These considerations outweigh the status of legal entities. There is also great complexity and interdependence in successfully conducting certain operations which are not easily understood by non-financial-sector people. In contrast, national fiscal authorities focus on legal entities and seek reassurance by discovering comparables.

The group has a long-standing relationship with the IRS and a growing interaction with the IR. Generally, tax enquiries are handled centrally but there are tax department specialists at the major subsidiaries who liaise with local inspectors. In total, the internal tax department numbers approximately 70, although these resources are not devoted entirely to transfer-pricing issues. However, dependent on whether a review or audit is under way, some senior tax personnel will be spending a quarter to a third of their time on transfer pricing. These will be the policy issues surrounding justification of the various methods because the record-keeping and documentation is effectively outsourced to the accounting controller's department. The resource commitment is therefore significant, and some growth in tax personnel is expected. However, this level of resourcing is needed to comply with the increasing tax regulations worldwide: 'We just haven't got the resources to start trying to fiddle around with things. It's such a mammoth task that it's not a[n effective] tax-avoidance tool to have transfer pricing.'

APAs

The APA concerns trading with ancillary services provided by an unregulated US swaps entity. One of the major points at issue over the three-year negotiations is the value of capital.

The group engaged a law firm and then briefed the IRS on its intentions, allowing it 3–4 months to digest the proposal. The Inland Revenue was also briefed informally, and six months later a formal submission for a bilateral APA to cover 1994–8 was made. Discussions with the IRS and IR continued separately but never with both authorities together. The competent authorities hold regular quarterly meetings where issues like this APA can be discussed.

When the IRS has considered an APA, a position paper is issued. The company can then respond to clarify or elaborate the IRS position or to question it. Copies of these are sent to the IR to keep it updated. A similar arrangement works when the company responds to the IR and a copy is sent to the IRS.

The legal advisers effectively manage the process. Having consulted with the company's management, the legal advisers interact with the IRS/IR and organise meetings where the advisers and group management will be present. The main legal adviser working on this APA for the group used to be head of the IRS APA process. Viewing an APA as a legal agreement naturally led to the selection of a US law firm and it is unknown whether such a service is currently available in the UK.

'The submission was to cover 1994–8 so, you know, we are still miles apart with six months to go, so whether it's true to call it an advance pricing agreement is a matter of viewpoint.' If agreement is needed, it is the company's hope that the APA will apply for similar transactions prior to 1994 and for at least three years after 1998. The time consumed by high-ranking management and external advisers created significant costs. If the way the company is organised and the transaction dealt with has not changed, the need for a new APA seems unwarranted.

All queries from the relevant fiscal authority initially come to the law firm and, despite submitting two thick lever-arch files to support the APA, several queries have been received – for example, the value of capital and enquiries about the opportunity cost of capital to the group; obtaining similar ancillary services but from an independent third party; and the location of the unregulated swaps entity, are all queries received from the IRS.

It should be remembered that the APA exclusively concerns the non-US-dollar swaps traded and managed out of London. The prospect of repeating the exercise for dollar/yen swaps, etc., and for other parts of the business is viewed with trepidation.

Managerial compensation and rewards

There is no direct or rigid link between, let us say, trader compensation and fees or profits recorded in a particular subsidiary. For coverage personnel, a longer-term view must be taken consistent with building client relationships. The investment in human capital is therefore significant and individuals with specific profiles, such as an ex-minister of an Eastern European country, may be recruited and retained. Likewise, expertise in a particular industry sector may mean that very few people are available who fit the profile. Retention is therefore important, and group management take conditions in this specialist labour market into account when rewarding and compensating staff.

The euro and year 2000 issues

These are seen as IT issues. Updating of systems is required and under way, but the impact on transfer-pricing policies is thought to be minimal. The main concern is to continue to demonstrate that expenses are shown in the right location.

The ultimate wish

The participating company would wish for a quick APA procedure. Experience in other US companies suggests 1½–3 years to obtain an APA, and the system has then generally worked. This group has encountered a particularly difficult case with its APA submission, but this does not detract from the potential benefits of having APAs. The US regulations are perceived as onerous, but there are signs that the fiscal authorities know more precisely which documents and functional analysis were required.

Themes

Acceptance of commercial reality and compliance costs by the fiscal authorities and, in exchange, the provision of full documentation by companies seems a recurring theme. The need to treat APAs as quasi-legal agreements may increase the costs but offers greater assurance and confidence for the company.

In financial services, policy issues surrounding transfer pricing are driven by fiscal considerations. The inherent complexity and interdependence of activities renders profit-centre management, except on a global or regional basis, extremely difficult. Hence, when investment in human capital is significant, financial performance measures play little part in rewarding effective managers.

Company 9

The specific transaction

The specific transaction relates to the UK head office management charges for the finance and marketing functions, which are charged out to different countries and tax jurisdictions. The group is divided into four main regions: the UK; the Americas; Continental Europe; and Asia Pacific. The charges are split across these four regions on the basis of head office time sheets, and then these charges are split by function across countries in each region in a less formal manner. These charges are made quarterly, biannually or annually, depending on the size of the charge and specific requirements of each subsidiary.

The group is also considering ways in which to remit higher levels of funds back to the UK at lower rates of tax – for instance, transfer pricing, dividends and royalties are all possible options. In the last case, if the group starts charging its subsidiaries a royalty for use of a brand name it must be able to ensure that these charges are separate from the management charges. At the moment, the UK company does, in fact, charge royalties for the use of certain trademarks or IT software to the USA. However, royalties are more likely to need a study to establish an appropriate royalty rate than management charges.

The objective is to recharge as much of these head office costs as possible. This is partly tax driven because of the UK's relatively low corporate income tax rate, but it is also an efficient way of remitting funds back to the UK. Generally, the group manages to charge out in excess of 60 per cent of the head office costs. These functions are charged out at cost because the amount of value added attributable to these services is limited owing to their nature (e.g. financial services; general management services; i.e. there exists a comparable local alternative which, given the current strength of sterling, is unlikely to be more expensive). Following lengthy discussions, the Inland Revenue has accepted that these services can be recharged at cost (the Inland Revenue would prefer a mark-up) as long as any marketing services or referrals, which do add value, are charged out with a mark-up (which has been determined to be a 12.5 per cent margin). One problem is that there are no available comparables or industry comparable, so this mark-up was agreed between the company and the Inland Revenue.

Occasionally, big global clients will be serviced primarily by one overseas subsidiary. In these cases (e.g. in Germany and the USA), the UK head office might be charged a management fee for these clients. Typically this will be netted off against the management charges being charged in the opposite direction.

One of the problem areas – or exceptions – is when an overseas subsidiary is running at a loss (e.g. Thailand). In these cases the UK head office would try to minimise the charges to these countries, because if they continued to pay management charges they might have to be recapitalised or financed with additional loans from the UK. To compound the problem, these subsidiaries are more likely to receive greater attention and time from head office staff. In the past, the group has had a number of loss-making subsidiaries for a variety of reasons (e.g. global recession;

start-up costs). The likelihood is that the Inland Revenue will not support this treatment in the future, so the group might have to review the allocation of costs differently.

Strong currency is a problem: it means that the group could not add mark-ups to services provided to overseas affiliates because they argue that they could source these services cheaper locally.

Acceptability of management charges

Some foreign subsidiaries do not like to receive management charges or complain that these charges are excessive. This concern is probably driven by the fact that these subsidiaries do not know the extent of the work or the real cost of the functions carried out by the UK head office. In terms of performance evaluation, companies and their management are assessed on their operating profit (revenues less operating costs). Apart from directly attributable costs, management charges are charged below the operating profit level.

Management charges have come under close scrutiny from the tax authorities in the USA, Australia and Germany, all of which require documentation to verify both that the UK head office has incurred costs and that these costs relate to the overseas jurisdiction. The group operates on the basis that if the Inland Revenue and the IRS can be satisfied, then a comparable level of documentation should be adequate for overseas tax jurisdictions.

APAs

At the moment the group has a satisfactory 'arrangement' with the Inland Revenue – in the form of verbal assurances (from the local business unit) covering the next two or three years. As long as the group maintains its documentation, it is unlikely that the benefits of an APA (or the potential costs associated with getting their policy wrong) will outweigh the costs of an APA. For instance, advisers' fees could easily be in the region of £50,000–100,000.

Tax expertise

The group tends to use tax advisers local to the subsidiaries' countries for many tax functions. The group's only tax professional is based in the UK and he deals with all matters relating to transfer pricing. In particular, documentation and any information relating to management charges are located in the UK head office. If there are any queries concerning transfer pricing in overseas jurisdictions, these will be dealt with by the UK head office.

> *If there is one aspect of ITP which would improve your level of assurance of meeting tax authority enquiries, what would it be?*
>
> I suppose the biggest bugbear is going to be the answer you will get from a lot of people, i.e. the amount of documentation that you have to keep. I think that once you have a policy which is acceptable to the local revenue authority, we

> would like to say we can use the same methodology on a worldwide basis and replicate the documentation. The provision of different documentation for different authorities is extremely time-consuming.

In addition, if there are disagreements over tax in countries which have tax treaties with the UK (the vast majority of the countries in which the group operate do have double taxation treaties with the UK), then there should be

> ... a method of resolving differences whereby these are resolved between authorities and do not actually need to involve us. As a result, from a commercial standpoint we could get on and do the rest of our job. I spend an awful lot of time doing transfer-pricing documentation and it is not a value-added exercise at all.

Euro

It will have an effect – the European management accounts will be prepared in euros from next year. However, management charges are invoiced in sterling and will continue to be invoiced in sterling.

Company 10

The specific transaction

The participating company is the UK subsidiary of a US parent whose main activity centres on the upstream oil business. Among other services, the UK subsidiary provides expertise on platform engineering, exploration in specific locations, and related issues to order, for the group and joint ventures.

Service arguments are used for both intra-group and joint-venture transactions. These incorporate transfer prices which are based on actual cost (budgeted figures are adjusted to actual at the year end) plus a mark-up. The process of cost accumulation involves identification of the UK subsidiary's office and staff costs, and overheads, plus any allocation of costs from the US parent. These costs are converted into hourly rates for different staff departments at the UK subsidiary. Considerable care is taken in this process because joint-venture partners are billed in the same way. Hence, for secretaries, engineers, accountants, etc., there will be an hourly rate for charge-out purposes. Overheads are allocated on traditional methods rather than ABC (activity-based costing).

The service agreements incorporate the hourly rates for the personnel committed to the service provision multiplied by the actual hours each department worked. The potentially contentious issue concerns the mark-up or profit element which is added to the service agreement. This is handled in a number of ways:

- documentation and accounting records are available to uphold the cost-accumulation process;
- service agreements with joint ventures and sister subsidiaries follow the same process of calculating hourly rates, which are consistently applied for the differing grades of personnel involved;
- well-established relationships with the OTO (Oil Taxation Office) of the IR International Division enable informal clearances to be offered and agreed in advance of the service agreements becoming operational.

This last point requires elaboration. In order for agreement to be reached on the mark-up, the participant's experience suggests that a 'reasonably solid proposal' is essential. This includes specifying the work to be done, the relationship of the parties and the transfer-price calculation. The OTO inspectors have knowledge of the industry and the practices of other countries, so that any negotiation on the mark-up is undertaken on an informed basis. In addition, it is felt that the OTO's knowledge base is strengthened by closer links with the IRS in more recent times. As the participant company states: 'I think the OTO likes to be seen to be commercial. If you go in with a commercial argument, they will normally follow it up.' Ultimately, if requested, the UK subsidiary would be able to show the time sheets for individuals who have contributed to specific service agreements. The process of determining the mark-up is the same for joint-venture and intra-group service agreements, although comparable uncontrolled prices cannot be identified because the combination of expertise and personnel skills varies with agreement. Nevertheless, having a well-documented, uniform process for the transfer-price calculation appears to create a good working relationship with the OTO in this case.

Exceptions

The specific series of transactions relates to service agreements only. In other areas, transfer pricing can be more contentious. Even with service agreements, certain jurisdictions outside the UK offer, say, one month's oil production or 20 per cent of the oil produced instead of the normal cost plus mark-up recovery agreement.

Managerial evaluation and rewards

Within this group, results are consolidated on a regional level. Technically, a subsidiary manager has the option of obtaining service agreements outside the group, but guaranteeing the same level of experienced advice without endangering commercial confidentiality may render this unfeasible. The aggregation of results to regions should mitigate against the transfer-pricing system having a major effect on the lower-level, subsidiary manager. Gaining assurance from the OTO that the service agreement is acceptable appears to be of greater importance.

Relationship with the OTO

The impending legislation in the UK and the publication of the Consultative Document have not noticeably altered the relationship with the OTO:

> I think from our perspective we have what I regard as a pretty decent relationship as far as services are concerned. It's difficult to see how they could be more accommodating, except on the level of the mark-up itself. We always have concerns about the mark-up's too high. But how do you get to it when you haven't got a market outside that you can compare?

The OTO is aware of and recognises commercial arguments in transfer-price-setting:

> ... the OTO appears to be working quite effectively as a collector but also as an adviser to the industry. Maybe the International Division should think about setting up one (equivalent to OTO) for financial services, etc.

Outsourcing of tax advice

At present the tax department in the UK subsidiary devotes 5 per cent of its time to transfer pricing in connection with service agreements. This may change with self-assessment but, in any event, having the specialist knowledge in-house is regarded as preferable to outsourcing. The industry is complex and dynamic, requiring specific knowledge of tax implications. It is unlikely that it would be cost-effective to expect this level of expertise from tax accountants outside the group.

Themes

Having well-established relationships with industry specialists in the IR appears to be important in agreeing transfer prices for service agreements. This trust is built and reinforced over time by having detailed records and clear processes to uphold this computation of transfer prices. Individual managerial responsibility as reflected by financial performance measures is of secondary consideration in operating effectively in this industry. Normally the company has to apply the required tax treatment – this is not very flexible.

Company 11

The specific transaction

The specific transaction relates to the non-dollar swap derivatives of a US group. Management control for this activity tends to lie outside the USA in London, Sydney, Tokyo, Singapore and Hong Kong. The main issues underlying this transaction include the location of risk, the location of capital, the business unit which generates the business and the business unit which executes the business.

The main risk-carrier is an unregulated US vehicle which makes agreement with other (lower credit rating) vehicles throughout the world. In recent years there has been an EU bank intermediary, separating the US and overseas vehicles, which was selected because it is in the EU and the group already has two banks in the UK (the other possibility considered outside the EU was Switzerland). In some instances, other parties prefer to deal with such a bank vehicle rather than the unregulated US vehicle. Of these two vehicles, the US one is the big risk-taker and the Irish bank is subject to some risk. For the role played by the EU bank it receives a credit intermediation fee – a measure of value at risk. But there are different views about what regulatory capital is required to cover which risks, dependent on whether a regulator or fiscal standpoint is taken. Also, what is the capital being used for? For example, in some countries the vehicles act only as an agent and the only capital required is to cover expenses, whereas in other countries the regulatory capital is used to carry all the risks.

As a separate activity, there is a AAA-rated European vehicle in another country which is remote from the risk and acts as a guarantor. This vehicle is remunerated in terms of a fee for that intermediation. The ultimate parent also provides a guarantee for all swaps business.

Transfer-pricing policy

A unilateral transfer-pricing agreement with the UK Inland Revenue has been in place since 1992–3. At that time, the group was discussing APAs with Japan, the USA and the UK. Eventually, a formal agreement was struck with the Inland Revenue which stated that the policy was believed to be acceptable to the IRS as well. It was agreed that the net profit could be divided into two elements – 50 per cent capital (how the balance sheet is used) and 50 per cent people (their expertise). There are very few comparables – companies prepared to allow their balance sheet to be used for writing swaps. However, existing comparables suggest that the third-party view of risk is that net profit should be divided into 80 per cent capital and 20 per cent people, but this is unacceptable to the Inland Revenue. The 80/20 split between capital and people is based on 'value at risk', in which the balance sheet has the major input (i.e. the name and rating of the group) and traders are less influential. However, this line of reasoning is less likely to be accepted by fiscal authorities.

Given the agreement about how net profit is apportioned, the derivation of net profit needs to be explained. Net profit equates to the global function's profit figure, adding back the fees paid to the business units around the world (computed on a cost-plus basis which varies for different countries), then subtracting the actual costs incurred by the business units (on a cost-only basis). This net profit figure is then apportioned in a slightly different way to the 50/50 split originally agreed, which reflects bargaining, and the new split has been agreed by the Inland Revenue. In actual fact, 55 per cent is for the capital element (or the parent company's guarantee) and 45 per cent is for the human element. In turn, this human element is weighted across five subheadings – 35 per cent: new deals or driven by where commissions arise; 25 per cent traders; 30 per cent salaries; 5 per cent for the key central management; and 5 per cent for the ultimate risk in the USA. In this equation, the traders effectively have double weighting as they are also included in salaries. It also recognises and rewards the originator of a deal (new deals) and the executor (traders).

In the UK company there are nineteen tax professionals, of whom two are full-time transfer-pricing specialists. There are about 60–90 internal agreements on transfer pricing.

Experience with the IRS

The group entered into the APA process with the IRS concerning a different transfer-pricing issue, but pulled out after 9–15 months of negotiations, dissatisfied with the process. The issue was not complex or difficult, but the group typically faced over twenty members of the IRS as part of the negotiation process. This team consisted of a Washington IRS team which appeared to understand the reason for the APA process, and a New York IRS team which appeared to want to learn as much about the group as possible.

In terms of structure, the IRS treats branches and permanent establishments (PEs) in exactly the same way – the same way as the UK Inland Revenue treats branches. In these instances, the host nation will argue that it is entitled to reward for both the people and the capital used in the branch. On the other hand, the Inland Revenue might not argue the same position for PEs in the UK (i.e. argue that there should be a reward for use of the capital in the UK).

Role of US law firms

In the USA, law firms sign off that an arm's-length price is reasonable. This facility provides the group with a letter of comfort, and it also means that the group is able to sue the law firm if the prices are not deemed acceptable by the fiscal authorities.

Management remuneration

The relationships between bonuses and the way in which profit is divided between business units is not necessarily transparent. For instance, profits might be very poor but a person might still receive very high bonuses because the company does not want to lose him/her. Alternatively, if a highly successful person is likely to leave the company anyway, there is no need to reward them with huge bonuses.

Each business unit is allocated a bonus pool on the basis of a variety of decisions, including which products the group wants to promote, but mainly profitability based on the business unit's P&L account after the transfer-pricing policy has been applied:

> Now there are decisions up here as to how much bonus pool goes to a particular business unit which will be affected by how we want to drive that product forward so we will enrich their bonus pool. That might pick up a new kind of product situation, might pick up a product when they want to push it very quickly.

The profitability will be affected by many strategic decisions: for instance, if the group acquires a new business, which business units should be charged with the cost of the acquisition or should the total cost be shared between a number of business units? Once a bonus pool has been allocated to each business unit, the bonuses will be shared out according to many different factors.

Changes in group structure

The parent guarantor currently receives a 55 per cent reward for its capital. As the corporate structure changes, additional regulated, well-capitalised entities are acting as intermediaries. Given that their guarantees are almost as good as the parent company, which vehicle should receive what part of the 55 per cent reward for capital? It is likely that the US parent company guarantee only applies in a scenario in which both the EU bank and the US unregulated vehicle go bust. If the guarantee is written in terms of this arrangement, the reward would be considerably less than the 55 per cent (perhaps as low as 1 per cent).

The location of these ultimate guarantees is an important aspect of the transfer-pricing policy. As individual affiliate banks improve their credit position, it is likely to change the location, which is rewarded for providing capital. These issues are important because: 'And that's a tension as we go forward because clearly that's a big way of swinging profitability into a low tax environment.'

The strategy of the group is also to move more business into regulated rather than unregulated entities: 'It's pushing our business more into regulated entities ... A conscious decision ... because the belief is that as we move forward, we will generally be required to do business within regulated entities.' For instance, the UK requires regulated bodies whereas the rules in the USA allow unregulated bodies. However, in the USA, unregulated bodies are not permitted to trade (e.g. in bonds) and this is why the equity derivatives business moved from an unregulated US vehicle to the UK.

Location decision

Both regulatory requirements and where business is generated drive location decisions:

- 'The management drivers as to where you're located come from a regulatory requirement. You may require in Italy, let's say, a regulated individual as part of an Italian legal entity to sell swaps to an Italian. You may require a legal entity in France to sell swaps. So those would be drivers at that level.'
- 'Obviously the drive would strongly come too from the sales side that ... until fairly recently a lot of the derivatives market was sold into Japan so clearly you're going to have a strong sales force in somewhere like that.'

Company 12

The specific transaction

This involves the provision of engineering services where the parent is based in the USA and a new subsidiary is established in India. The location in India is partially based on strategic considerations such as the quality of employees and the nearness of markets like Russia and the CIS and the Near East. Transfer pricing was not, however, a part of the FDI decision except after the subsidiary became operational.

Certainly the location of a services subsidiary in a low-cost country influenced the FDI but, of equal importance, the level of education, relatively unsophisticated tax rules and the low cost of investment played a role. In some respects the start-up costs, including the need to relocate five ex-patriate experts, contributed more to the creation costs than any investment in physical assets.

A wholly-owned subsidiary was established in accordance with Indian law, which does not allow the creation of branches for this industry. Equity investment was not contemplated because 'repatriation of equity was virtually impossible' and 'foreign exchange restrictions make dividend redistribution very difficult (although subsequent deregulation eased the requirements)'. The benefit to the host government of the subsidiary operating there was based on (a) hi-tech training being available to indigenous Indians, and (b) if successful, foreign currency would flow to the host country. For the group, the establishment of a low-cost business unit in this location offered many attractions. In any event, investment in terms of loan capital enabled easier repatriation.

It must be acknowledged that other subsidiaries within the group offered engineering services to other subsidiaries. The investment required a recognition of capacity, i.e. man-hours, and costs in order that contracts awarded worldwide could rely on the Indian subsidiary's low costs. By incorporating the Indian services, more competitive tendering or more profitable contracts could be obtained. Within the group the Indian subsidiary transfer price provided an economic benchmark for other subsidiaries.

Internally, a 'commercial team' is responsible for cost build-ups to tender for contracts. Once successful, a project manager is appointed who then decides, within the overall budget, which subsidiaries will provide which services. Whichever business unit or subsidiary is selected, a transfer price will be used. Even though the Indian subsidiary price may have been incorporated in the tender, there is no necessity for the project manager to use that subsidiary. The commercial team will undoubtedly take into account the cost of using the Indian subsidiary, while risk factors associated with where the work is to be executed and an appropriate profit margin have to be taken into account. There is also the consideration of 'what the customer is actually going to accept or what the competitors are bidding'. For a start-up subsidiary, the transfer price for engineering services may therefore have varied with the project, industry, market and the different risk factors involved. However, to keep the administrative costs manageable, it was decided that the Indian subsidiary would charge a standard per hour transfer price.

In terms of rewarding project managers, profit after indirect but before direct tax was the essential bottom-line target. Customs duties were a project cost, but not income tax, so the tax department had to educate or persuade project managers to follow actions that minimised income taxes, even if some extra indirect taxes resulted. The persuasion was aided by the group bonus scheme being based on group after-tax profit. Senior VPs of operations are then responsible to recognise the performance of project managers. The tax department was able to persuade project managers that locating the appropriate profit after tax in the relevant location aided the group and their performance-related rewards, even though before-tax project profit may be reduced. Hence, relationships between project managers and the tax department were built.

The tax department, after the awarding of any contract, had a significant influence over the intercompany transfer prices to be charged. However, the Indian subsidiary was a special case. Having decided to operate from this location and to avoid high administration costs by charging a fixed per hour charge-out rate, the main aim was to keep profits in India low, given the Indian government's repatriation restrictions, etc.

The transfer price was set at a level which would have created a loss for the first two years of the start-up and then gradually to show a profit in years 3 and 4. In several respects this is realistic, given that effective training and acceptance by other parts of the group take time. Also, a single charge-out rate offers simplicity and straightforwardness for the Indian fiscal authorities, and the benefit of tax loss carry-overs may be utilised in future years. From the group's point of view, the transfer price for engineering services from India provided a benchmark which other subsidiaries had to meet or better.

The problems with the transfer-pricing policy became apparent during the third year of operation. For two years, losses at the Indian subsidiary had been reported. It became apparent that the uniform transfer price was the problem. It had been determined based on a forecast level of activity that had not in fact been attained. Project managers were not using the Indian subsidiary due to concerns about the quality of work.

From a tax viewpoint, they needed to increase the transfer price to enable the subsidiary to show profits. However, from a worldwide business perspective, there was a strong desire on the part of senior management to build the Indian office and increase the experience and training for the local staff. Any increase in the price charged by the Indian subsidiary would create a further disincentive to project managers to use the Indian operation.

Hence, it was agreed that two sets of accounts were to be kept in future. The subsidiary manager would be performing well if break-even and utilisation rates met expectations. The transfer-pricing rate was increased for local and taxation reporting in order that a positive turnaround situation could be shown in the latter half of year 3. The group therefore issued, officially, invoices for the engineering services of India which formed part of the local tax reporting, but different transfer prices for the internal management report. The latter offered conformity and comparison between parts of the group, enabling top management to make strategic decisions. The former allowed the group to be open with the local tax authorities.

Relationship with tax authorities

Group policy is to rely on local accounting firms for normal compliance work. There are also likely to be advisers who interface with fiscal authorities rather than relying on employees of the group. Employees are not allowed to speak with local tax authorities (except in well-developed countries such as the USA and the UK), and the regional or central tax department is required to review an overseas set of accounts before they are filed.

In the event of an enquiry or investigation-type query, the central or regional tax department will liaise with the overseas advisers.

Over the last 40 years, the group has developed a well-established relationship with the IRS, consistent with most large US companies – a representative has a permanent room at HQ in the USA. Reviews and liaison have therefore been commonplace and the need for APAs is perceived as minimal.

However, if a project is large enough, and in jurisdictions where experience is limited, then a ruling with the relevant tax authority will be obtained. This is crucial when untried structures/relationships are employed under developing tax regimes.

Themes

Transfer pricing is a post-event consideration in FDI decisions. It is used to balance managerial motivation with corporate post-tax expectations. Central/HQ tax expertise enables strategic decisions to be fulfilled to their full potential, although two sets of performance metrics may be needed.

Implementing structures and carrying out actions which are tax-efficient from an overall group perspective require relationship-building with relevant staff, who need to be persuaded to do the right thing for the group, even though no direct personal benefit is derived (and in some cases they need to 'put themselves out' to do something).

Appendix 2: Survey Instrument

Transfer Pricing

A strictly confidential survey – all responses will remain anonymous.

Compiled by: Jamie Elliott, Lecturer in Accounting at the University of Southampton. Sponsored by: The Chartered Institute of Management Accountants (CIMA) and supported by Deloitte & Touche.

Self-assessment for transfer pricing

The recent Inland Revenue Consultative Document proposed draft transfer-pricing regulations to be implemented as part of the move to self-assessment in the UK. When signing the annual tax return, a company representative will be implicitly confirming that the declared profits are computed according to the arm's-length standard. Penalties of up to 100 per cent of the tax lost will be payable on negligent or fraudulent returns.

This survey presents both foreign-owned companies and UK groups with an opportunity to respond to self-assessment in particular and to some highly topical transfer-pricing issues in general.

Your help is greatly appreciated. It should take no more than 20 minutes to complete the survey, and a stamped, addressed envelope is enclosed.

If you would like to receive a copy of the overall findings and would be prepared to contribute further, please give details of a contact address:

Name: ______________________________

Address: ______________________________

____

Contact telephone no. ______________________________

Further contribution (Yes/No) ______________________________

Please reply to:

Jamie Elliott
Department of Management
University of Southampton
Highfield
Southampton SO17 1BJ
Tel: 01703-594738 Fax: 01703-593844
E-mail: je2@soton.ac.uk

SECTION 1

ORGANISATIONAL CHARACTERISTICS

1a. What is the level of annual company sales?

Less than £100 million ________
£100m < sales < £250m ________
£250m < sales < £500m ________
£500m < sales < £1000m ________
£1000m < sales < £2500m ________
£2500m < sales < £5000m ________
Over £5000m ________

1b. Is your company the parent company?

Yes _____ No _____

1c. Is your company the European headquarters company of the worldwide group?

Yes _____ No _____

1d. In which country is your ultimate parent company incorporated?

____

2. What is the nature of the company's activity?

Wholesaler ________
Distributor ________
Retailer ________
Manufacturer ________
Service company ________
R&D facility ________
Banking/investment ________
Other ________________

3a. What is the proportion of internal trade (i.e. with other group companies) as a percentage of total company sales?

Less than 1% ________
1% < proportion < 10% ________
10% < proportion < 25% ________
25% < proportion < 50% ________
Greater or equal to 50% ________

3b. What is the proportion of *international* internal trade (i.e. with other group companies in different countries) as a percentage of total company sales?

Less than 1% ________
1% < proportion < 10% ________
10% < proportion < 25% ________
25% < proportion < 50% ________
Greater or equal to 50% ________

4a. What is your *single main/predominant type of international internal transaction?*

____

____

4b. What are the characteristics of your *single main/predominant international internal transaction?* (as specified in 4b)

	Non-specific				Highly specific
Human/capital Investment	1	2	3	4	5
	Occasional				Recurring
Frequency	1	2	3	4	5
	Very low				Very high
Volumes	1	2	3	4	5
	Very uncertain				Very certain
Levels of certainty	1	2	3	4	5

5. What constraints are placed on a buying division's decision to buy externally (rather than internally)?
Please circle:

No constraints				Totally constrained
1	2	3	4	5

6. How appropriate are these descriptions of your company's operations?
Please circle:

	Not at all appropriate				Very appropriate
Vertically integrated	1	2	3	4	5
Diversified	1	2	3	4	5
Technologically sensitive	1	2	3	4	5
Speciality products with no intermediate market	1	2	3	4	5
Predominantly UK presence	1	2	3	4	5

7a. Have you recorded trading losses in any of the last 3 financial years?

Yes _____ No _____

7b. If YES to 7a, what is this due to?

Local competition _________
Start-up _________
Exchange rate _________
Poor product _________
Transfer pricing _________
Other _________
Other _________

SECTION 2

TRANSFER PRICING

8. Does your company use the same method of transfer pricing for both domestic and international transfers?

Yes _____ No ______

9. How have your dealings with the UK tax authorities on transfer-pricing issues changed over the last 3 years?

Much more uncertain		No change		Much more certain
1	2	3	4	5

10. What are the main transfer-pricing issues in your company? Please circle:

In general terms:

	Never	Infrequently	Sometimes	Often	Always
•Goods	1	2	3	4	5
•Services	1	2	3	4	5
•Intangibles	1	2	3	4	5
•Financing	1	2	3	4	5

More specifically:

	Never	Infrequently	Sometimes	Often	Always
•Commissions	1	2	3	4	5
•Debt/equity structure	1	2	3	4	5
•Expense allocation	1	2	3	4	5
•Information technology expenditure	1	2	3	4	5
•interest expense allocation	1	2	3	4	5
•Interest paid on intra-group loans	1	2	3	4	5
•Intra-group transfer of technology and other intangibles	1	2	3	4	5
•Management fees	1	2	3	4	5
•Permanent establishments	1	2	3	4	5
•R&D	1	2	3	4	5
•Royalty valuation	1	2	3	4	5
•Service fees	1	2	3	4	5

Please specify others:

_________	1	2	3	4	5
_________	1	2	3	4	5

11. Is it possible to identify a comparable arm's-length transaction in your industry? Please circle:

Not at all				To a great extent
1	2	3	4	5

12. Using OECD terminology, do you use the following methods within your organisation? Please circle:

	Never	Infrequently	Sometimes	Often	Always
Comparable uncontrolled price (CUP)	1	2	3	4	5
Resale price	1	2	3	4	5
Cost-plus	1	2	3	4	5
Profit-split	1	2	3	4	5
Comparable profits method (CPM)	1	2	3	4	5
Transactional net margin method (TNMM)	1	2	3	4	5

13. Please rank the top 3 pricing methods in order of applicability to your company (where 1 represents the most suitable).

	Rank
•CUP	_________
•Resale price	_________
•Cost-plus	_________
•Profit-split	_________
•CPM	_________
•TNMM	_________
Others:	
______________	_________
______________	_________

14. Do you use the following transfer-pricing methods in your company? Please circle:

	Never	Infrequently	Sometimes	Often	Always
Variable cost	1	2	3	4	5
Variable cost-plus	1	2	3	4	5
Full cost	1	2	3	4	5
Full cost-plus	1	2	3	4	5
Resale price	1	2	3	4	5
Resale–minus price	1	2	3	4	5

Market-based:

current price	1	2	3	4	5
adjusted	1	2	3	4	5

Others:

__________	1	2	3	4	5
__________	1	2	3	4	5

15. How important are the following factors in your company for the determination of a transfer price? Please circle:

	Very unimportant		Neutral		Very important
Internal Factors:					
•Competitive position of foreign subsidiary	1	2	3	4	5
•Consistency with the computer systems for producing internal accounts	1	2	3	4	5
•Cross-subsidisation	1	2	3	4	5
•Local market conditions	1	2	3	4	5
•Maintain solvency of subsidiary	1	2	3	4	5
•Market penetration	1	2	3	4	5
•Motivate local manage-ment	1	2	3	4	5
•Parent cost recovery	1	2	3	4	5
•Provide a subsidiary with a fair return on assets	1	2	3	4	5
•Provide the parent with a fair return on assets	1	2	3	4	5
•Simplicity and ease of use	1	2	3	4	5
•Stability of transfer price over time	1	2	3	4	5
•Subsidiary performance evaluation	1	2	3	4	5
•Subsidisation of infant foreign subsidiary	1	2	3	4	5
•Other: __________	1	2	3	4	5
External Factors:					
•Aggressiveness of tax authority	1	2	3	4	5
•Differentials in tax rates and tax legislation among countries	1	2	3	4	5
•Maximisation of global profit	1	2	3	4	5
•Parent country's tax treatment of dividend remittances	1	2	3	4	5
•Protection against foreign exchange losses	1	2	3	4	5
•Rate of customs duties and legislation	1	2	3	4	5
•Tax structure within the European Union	1	2	3	4	5
•UK tax treatment of dividend remittances	1	2	3	4	5
•Other: __________	1	2	3	4	5

16. Please rank the top 3 factors (from qu. 15) in order of importance to your company in determining the transfer price. (1 = most important; 3 = third most important.)

•Competitive position of foreign subsidiary __________
•Consistency with the computer systems for producing internal accounts __________
•Cross-subsidisation __________
•Local market conditions __________
•Maintain solvency of subsidiary __________

•Market penetration __________
•Motivate local management __________
•Parent cost recovery __________
•Provide a subsidiary with a fair return on assets __________
•Provide the parent with a fair return on assets __________
•Simplicity and ease of use __________
•Stability of transfer price over time __________
•Subsidiary performance evaluation __________
•Subsidisation of infant foreign subsidiary __________
•Aggressiveness of tax authority __________

•Differentials in tax rates and tax legislation among countries __________
•Maximisation of global profit __________
•Parent country's tax treatment of dividend remittances __________
•Protection against foreign exchange losses __________
•Rate of customs duties and legislation __________
•Tax structure within the European Union __________
•UK tax treatment of dividend remittances __________

•Other: ______________________________

•Other: ______________________________

17. To what extent are managers in your company involved in pricing decisions regarding the internal transfer of goods?

	Not involved				Highly involved	N/A
a) Imports from the parent company	1	2	3	4	5	0
b Imports from other group affiliates	1	2	3	4	5	0
c) Exports to the parent company	1	2	3	4	5	0
d) Exports to other group affiliates	1	2	3	4	5	0

18a. Has your company been the subject of an Inland Revenue transfer-pricing audit in the last 5 years? Please tick:

Yes _____ No ______

18b. If your answer to 18a) was YES:

What areas did the transfer-pricing audit concentrate on/query?

____

____

18c. Was there a subsequent adjustment? Please tick:

Yes _____ No ______

19a. Please specify any other countries in which your company has been the subject of a transfer-pricing audit in the last 5 years?

____

____

____

19b. What areas did the transfer-pricing audit concentrate on/query?

____

____

____

19c. Was there a subsequent adjustment? Please tick:

Yes _____ No _____

20. How important do you consider the possibility of obtaining an advanced pricing ruling for your company? Please circle:

Very unimportant		Neutral		Very important
1	2	3	4	5

SECTION 3

SELF-ASSESSMENT

21. Would you be confident in certifying that your organisation's tax returns are in accordance with the arm's-length standard?

Please circle as appropriate:

a) Confident

b) Generally confident, certain minor transactions require review

c) Concerned, one fundamenta transaction group requires review

d) Extremely concerned, the majority of transaction groups require review

Comments:

22. The Consultative Document proposed that contemporaneous documentation is required to demonstrate compliance with the arm's-length standard. Do you retain transfer-pricing documentation for:

Please circle as appropriate:

a) All transactions

b) Just for the major transactions

c) Transactions covered by previous internal reviews

d) Limited documentation, only if prepared for other business purposes

e) No documentation

Comments :

23. Are you aware of the documentation requirements set out in the proposed legislation?

Please circle as appropriate:

a) Yes

b) No

Comments :

24. Do you consider you have the resources in-house to prepare the necessary contemporaneous documentation?

Please circle as appropriate:

a) Yes

b) Yes, considering final review by the professional adviser

c) No, require some assistance from professional adviser

d) No, will engage full transfer-pricing study from professional adviser

Comments :

25. Have you considered the likely compliance costs of implementing the new transfer-pricing legislation?

Please circle as appropriate:

a) No

b) Yes £0–£49,999

c) Yes £50,000–£99,999

d) Yes £100,000–£149,999

e) Yes £150,000 plus

26. The requirement to declare the profits included in the tax return as arm's length will be introduced on the effective date for self-assessment (i.e. for financial years ending in 1999 onwards). Do you consider your organisation to be:

Please circle as appropriate:

a) Ready

b) Not yet prepared – plan in place to meet implementation date

c) Not yet prepared – currently drafting implementation plan

d) Not yet prepared – no implementation plan

Comments:

27. Who will be signing the tax return(s) in your organisation ?

Please circle as appropriate:

a) Tax manager/director

b) Financial controller

c) Financial director

d) Managing director/chief executive

e) Other: ______________________________

SECTION 4

TRANSFER-PRICING POLICY REVIEWS

28. When did your company have its most recent transfer-pricing policy review?

29. Who/which parts of the group determined the most recent transfer-pricing policy?

30. Who/which parts of the group were consulted as part of the most recent transfer-pricing policy review?

31. What were the main products/ activities addressed in the most recent transfer-pricing policy review?

32. What were the main problems encountered in the course of the most recent transfer-pricing policy review?

33. What were the main successes resulting from the most recent transfer-pricing policy review ?

Additional comments:

Thank you very much for participating in this research study.

Please return this questionnaire to Jamie Elliott in the stamped, addressed envelope provided.

References

Abdallah, W.M. (1989), *International Transfer Pricing Policies: Decision Making Guidelines for Multinational Companies,* Quorum Books.

Borkowski, S.C. (1992), 'Section 482, revenue procedure 91–22 and the realities of multinational transfer pricing', *International Tax Journal,* Spring 59–68.

Borkowski, S.C. (1996), 'An Analysis (Meta- and Otherwise) of Multinational Transfer Pricing', *International Journal of Accounting,* Vol. 31, No. 1, 39–53.

Colbert, G.J. and Spicer, B.H. (1995), 'A Multi-Case Investigation of a Theory of the Transfer Pricing Process', *Accounting, Organisations and Society,* Vol. 20, No. 6, 423–56.

Collins, J.H and Shackelford, D.A. (1998), 'Global Organisations and Taxes: An Analysis of the Dividend, Interest, Royalty, and Management Fee Payments between US Multinationals' Foreign Affiliates', *Journal of Accounting and Economics,* Vol. 24, 151–73.

Deloitte Touche Tohmatsu (1998), 'International Transfer Pricing', Deloitte, Touche Tohmatsu, January–April.

Deloitte Touche Tohmatsu (1999), 'Strategy Matrix for Global Transfer Pricing: Comparison of Methods, Documentation, Penalties, and Other Issues', 1 January.

Drury, J.C. (1996), *Management and Cost Accounting,* Boston: International Thomson Business Press.

Dunning, J.H. (1980), 'Towards an Eclectic Theory of International Production', *Journal of International Business Studies,* Vol. 11, Spring/Summer, No. 1, 9–31.

Dunning, J.H. (1981), *International Production and the Multinational Enterprise,* London: Allen and Unwin.

Dunning, J.H. (1988), *Explaining International Production,* London: Allen and Unwin.

Dunning, J.H. and Pearce, R. (1995), *Comparative International Accounting, 4th edn,* London: Prentice Hall.

Eccles, R. G. (1985), *The Transfer Pricing Problem: A Theory for Practice,* Lexington, Mass. Heath.

Eisenhardt, K.M. (1989), 'Building Theories from Case Study Research', *Academy of Management Review,* Vol. 14, 532–50.

Elliott, J. (1998), *International Transfer Pricing: A Survey of UK and non-UK Groups,* London: CIMA Publishing.

Elliott, J. (1999), *Managing International Transfer Pricing Policies: A Grounded Theory Study,* PhD Thesis, University of Glasgow, May.

Emmanuel, C.R. and Mehafdi, M. (1994), *Transfer Pricing,* London: CIMA/Academic Press.

Emmanuel, C.R. and Mehafdi, M. (1998), 'An Investigation of Empirical Research in

Transfer Pricing', European Accounting Association 21st Annual Congress, Antwerp, 6–8 April.

GAO (1995), 'International Taxation – Transfer Pricing and Information on Non-payment of Tax', Report to Congressional Requesters, GAO/GGD-95 101, April, US General Accounting Office.

Giovannini, A., Hubbard, R.G. and Slemrod, J. (eds) (1993), *Studies in International Taxation*, Chicago: NBER/University of Chicago.

Grubert, H. and Mutti, J. (1991), 'Taxes, Tariffs and Transfer Pricing in Multinational Corporate Decision Making', *Review of Economics and Statistics* Vol. 73, May, 285–93.

Harris, D.G. (1993), 'The Impact of US Tax Law Revision on Multinational Corporations' Capital Location and Income-Shifting Decisions', *Journal of Accounting Research*, Vol. 31 (Suppl.), 1993, 111–40.

Hirshleifer, J. (1956), 'On the Economics of Transfer Pricing', *Journal of Business*, Vol. 29, 172–84.

Jacob, J. (1996), 'Taxes and Transfer Pricing: Income Shifting and the Volume of Intrafirm Transfers', *Journal of Accounting Research*, Vol. 34, No. 2, Autumn, 301–12.

Klassen, K., Lang, M. and Wolfson, M. (1993), 'Geographic Income Shifting by Multinational Corporations in Response to Tax Rate Changes', *Journal of Accounting Research*, Vol. 31 (Suppl.), 141–73.

Laster, D.S. and McCauley, R.N. (1994), 'Making Sense of the Profits of Foreign Firms in the United States', *Federal Reserve Bank of New York Quarterly Review*, Summer–Fall, 44–75.

Leitch, R.A. and Barrett, K.S. (1992), 'Multinational Transfer Pricing: Objectives and Constraints', *Journal of Accounting Literature*, Vol. 11, 47–92.

McAulay, L. and Tomkins, C.R. (1992), 'A Review of the Contemporary Transfer Pricing Literature with Recommendations for Future Research', *British Journal of Management*, Vol. 3, 101–22.

Meer-Kooistra, J. van der (1994), 'The Coordination of Internal Transactions: The Functioning of Transfer Pricing Systems in the Organisational Context', *Management Accounting Research*, Vol. 5, No. 2, June, 123–52.

Mehafdi, M. and Emmanuel, C.R. (1997), 'Convergence, Divergence in Transfer Pricing Research: A Forty-year Survey', Department of Accounting and Finance, University of Glasgow, Working Paper 97/9.

Merchant, K.A. (1997), *Modern Management Control Systems*, Prentice-Hall.

OECD (1994), 'Transfer Pricing Guidelines for Multinational Enterprises and Tax Administrations', *Discussion Draft of Part I: Principles and Methods*, Report of the OECD Committee on Fiscal Affairs, Paris.

Rugman, A.M. and Eden, L. (eds) (1985), *Multinationals and Transfer Pricing*, Croom Helm Series in International Business,. London: Croom Helm.

Scapens, R.W. (1990), 'Research Management Accounting Practice: The Role of Case Study Methods', *British Accounting Review*, Vol. 22, 259–81.

Spicer, B.H. (1988), 'Towards an Organisational Theory of the Transfer Pricing

Process', *Accounting, Organisations and Society,* Vol. 13, No. 3, 303–22.

Spicer, B.H. (1992), 'The Resurgence of Cost and Management Accounting: A Review of Some Recent Developments in Practice, Theories and Case Research Methods', *Management Accounting Research,* Vol. 3, 1–37.

Stitt, I. (1995), 'Transfer Pricing for the Next Century', *Accountancy,* November, 92–94.

Tang, R.Y.W. (1993), *Transfer Pricing Practices in the 1990s,* Quorum Books.

UNCTAD (1997a), 'World Investment Report – Transnational Corporations, Market Structure and Competition Policy', New York and Geneva: United Nations.

UNCTAD (1997b), 'World Investment Report – Transnational Corporations, Market Structure and Competition Policy: Overview', New York and Geneva: United Nations.

US (1994), *Internal Revenue Service Final Regulations* (TD 8552), Relating to Intercompany Transfer Pricing under Section 482.

Yin, R.K. (1989), *Case Study Research,* London: Sage Publications.